#TREATYOURSELF!

#TREATYOURSELF!

365 WAYS TO BE *happy every day*

GAIL RUSSELL

Avon, Massachusetts

Published by
Adams Media, a division of F+W Media, Inc.
57 Littlefield Street, Avon, MA 02322. U.S.A.
www.adamsmedia.com

Contains material adapted and abridged from An Indulgence a Day by
Andrea Norville and Patrick Menton, copyright © 2009 by F+W Media, Inc.,
ISBN 10: 1-60550-152-2, ISBN 13: 978-1-60550-152-9.

ISBN 10: 1-4405-8444-3
ISBN 13: 978-1-4405-8444-2
eISBN 10: 1-4405-8445-1
eISBN 13: 978-1-4405-8445-9

Printed in the United States of America.

10 9 8 7 6 5 4 3 2

Many of the designations used by manufacturers and sellers to distinguish
their products are claimed as trademarks. Where those designations appear
in this book and F+W Media, Inc. was aware of a trademark claim, the designations have been printed with initial capital letters.

Readers are urged to take all appropriate precautions before undertaking any
how-to task. Always read and follow instructions and safety warnings for all
tools and materials, and call in a professional if the task stretches your abilities too far. Although every effort has been made to provide the best possible
information in this book, neither the publisher nor the author is responsible
for accidents, injuries, or damage incurred as a result of tasks undertaken by
readers. This book is not a substitute for professional services.

Cover design by Frank Rivera.
Cover images © Iryna Matsiash/Elena Ivanova/happymay/123RF.

This book is available at quantity discounts for bulk purchases.
For information, please call 1-800-289-0963.

Introduction

We all enjoy doing nice things for others. Whether it's saving the last cookie for your husband or bringing a latte to your coworker when you know she's having a tough day, it feels good to help those we care about.

But what about you? In between the bustle of day-to-day life and the time you spend taking care of others, do you overlook yourself? If you have to think about it, the answer is yes.

Now's the time to give yourself some of that TLC you give to your loved ones. And indulging in a doughnut at a morning meeting only to feel guilty about it ten minutes later? That doesn't count—not even close.

Treating yourself is about doing something for you, without the guilt trip. Why not open that bottle of special-occasion champagne on a Tuesday afternoon? Who says you can't watch the sunrise and sunset in one day? When else will you take that cooking class you've always thought about?

The idea behind this book is simple: You deserve to be happy, and there are big and small ways to give yourself a shot of joy every day. From little things like having breakfast for dinner to grand gestures such as splurging for a "just because" night away, *#TreatYourself!* is filled with ways you can take care of you. After all, between work and taking care of those around you, you've earned the right to indulge!

We only get one life, so you might as well make the most of it. What are you waiting for? It's time to treat yourself.

1 *Make Snow Cones with Fresh Snow*

It can be difficult to find fun things to do in the dead of winter. However, there is one thing that you probably have more than enough of, so why not use it to your advantage. You're never too old for a snow cone, and what better way to treat yourself after a day of shoveling. Grab a bowl and a big spoon and collect some fresh, clean snow (it's best right after a storm). When you've filled your bowl, leave it in your freezer while you prepare the other ingredients. If you don't have any fresh snow or are concerned about acid rain, feel free to shave some ice in a blender. You can either buy some syrup flavoring at your local grocery store or make your own using a few simple ingredients. You will need:

8 ounces light corn syrup
Packet Kool-Aid powder
Water
Sugar (optional)

Pour the corn syrup into a cup. Add half of the packet of your favorite Kool-Aid powder. Add water (about 2–4 ounces) to the mixture until the powder and syrup are diluted. Add more Kool-Aid powder or sugar to taste. For fun, fill a martini glass with snow from the freezer and pour the syrup over the snow.

This can be a fun activity to involve the kids in, but if there are no kids around, make your snow cone extra special by adding a shot of vodka or your favorite flavored liqueur into the syrup mixture. That's sure to relieve the winter blues!

. . . .

2 *Take a Sick Day for Sex*

Did you know that one-third of all employed U.S. adults do not take all of the vacation days they receive each year? If there is one reason to take a day off in the middle of the week, it's to have sex. Convince your sweetie to stay home, too, so you can enjoy each other all day long. If you haven't had morning sex since before going to class in college, go for it and follow up with breakfast in bed. Kill two birds with one stone, and make love in the shower. If you work a typical 9-to-5 job, you rarely get to have sex in the afternoon, unless you are really taking advantage of your lunch breaks. Your energy level will probably be at top performance, so get busy. If you've been doing it all day and need a break, use the nighttime to take a warm bath together and cuddle. This type of indulgence is a wonderful way to reconnect with your lover. Try to do it more than once a year. If you happen to be solo on your day off . . . enjoy the pleasure of your own company.

3 Make Your Own Sugar Body Scrub

Walk into any body-care shop and you'll find an array of salt and sugar scrubs that cost $20–$40 for one small jar. Exfoliating your skin doesn't have to be expensive. With a few simple ingredients you probably already have in your pantry, you can have a big batch of sweet-smelling scrub ready and waiting for you. You will need:

1 cup brown sugar
1 cup white sugar
Almond oil or vegetable oil
Essential oil or fragrance oil (try lemon or vanilla)

Mix the brown and white sugars in a medium-sized mixing bowl. Add the almond or vegetable oil to the sugar until it becomes a thick paste. Add a few drops of your favorite essential or fragrance oil. Try lemon, vanilla, lavender, or rose oil. Make sure you aren't allergic to any of the oils you want to use.

Jump in the shower and rub the mixture all over your body, paying close attention to typically dry areas like elbows and feet. It will not only leave you feeling soft and smooth, it will make you smell divine! The combinations for fragrances are endless. You can even make personalized sugar scrubs for your friends and family during the holidays or for birthdays.

4 Host a Dinner Party with Your Favorite Film As the Theme

Planning a meal for a group of people might raise your anxiety, but choosing foods based on your favorite film will make it more of an adventure than a chore. If you love *Casablanca*, serve traditional Moroccan fare, like roasted lamb and couscous. If *Forrest Gump* is more your style, serve a variety of shrimp dishes—take some ideas from Bubba's long list of recipes. If you want some help in the kitchen, turn your party into a potluck and let your friends know what the movie will be ahead of time. Having everyone come up with their own idea for a dish will add to the fun. If there is time after dinner, play the movie for your guests, and don't forget the popcorn!

5 Have Lunch in the Park

Getting out of the office for a lunch break is one of the most important things to do during the day. You need to get away to recharge your battery and refocus, even if it's just for a thirty-minute lunch break. The quickest way to get some relaxation is to find a park that is close to work and have a picnic for yourself. Before you leave for work in the morning, or even the night before, pack a picnic basket with a lunch you can look forward to all day. A grilled chicken salad with baby spinach, strawberries, and blueberries is not only delicious, but also offers protein and important antioxidants. Remember to pack some healthy snacks that will give you a much-needed boost of energy during the last half of the day. Bring tangerines or clementines for a quick burst of energy and some toasted almonds or cashews for long-lasting energy. Don't forget to add something a little decadent like a chocolate cupcake or a few oatmeal raisin cookies. Sit in the sun and close your eyes. Forget what you have to do when you get back to work; just enjoy your time away from the office. This is something you can do every day to treat yourself right.

. . . .

6 Take a Morning Walk

Start your day off right with a brisk thirty-minute walk first thing in the morning. Early in the morning, before everyone is awake and the sun is just starting to rise, is the best time. Many people find it to be the most spiritual part of the day. Take this time to meditate and prepare for the day ahead. It's a great way to allow your mind to relax, and not only will you feel refreshed and centered, but you will find that you have more energy throughout the day. Listen to some soothing music, or if you want to get your blood flowing bring some dance or techno music. It has also been shown that if you have a difficult time exercising consistently, doing so in the morning will make it easier to follow your routine. Make sure to eat a healthy breakfast when you return from your walk.

7 Start a Vacation Savings Account

With the rising cost of gas and food prices, planning a vacation is probably the last thing you can afford. It might seem like you will never be able to save for a getaway. However, if you can put just $20 a week into a high-yield savings account or even in a jar under the bed, you'll be surprised at how quickly it adds up. If $20 a week is more than you can afford, just put in what you can. You can even add the change left in your pockets at the end of the week. Being able to get away from your everyday life will be worth it.

8 Have an Afternoon Tea Party

There is something very elegant and relaxing about having afternoon tea. In the UK, where afternoon tea originated, tea time is traditionally between 3 P.M. and 5 P.M. Invite some friends over and have them wear lace gloves to add to the sense of occasion. If it is nice outside, serve tea in the garden. Offer a variety of teas like chamomile, Earl Grey, and peppermint. Don't forget the little cucumber sandwiches, cookies, and scones.

9 Buy a Removable Showerhead

For those of you that may not know, a removable showerhead can be used for reasons other than getting you clean. Take some time during your next shower to get up close and personal with the pulsating jets of water. Many of the showerheads available now offer different rates of speed and water pressure. Find the one you like the best and enjoy, with or without a partner.

10 Have Thanksgiving Dinner in the Spring

Thanksgiving is the one day of the year you can really indulge without worrying about the calories. Why wait until November to enjoy turkey and all the trimmings? Have a Thanksgiving feast in April or May. If you think the meal seems too heavy for the spring weather, make a few substitutions. Instead of butternut squash and mashed potatoes, try lighter vegetables like string beans and summer squash. Pumpkin pie is a must, though.

11 Brighten Up Your Workspace with Flowers

Whether we're sitting in the corner office or manning a cash register, everyone finds themselves watching the clock at work at one time or another. Brighten up your day and spread a little cheer to those around you by bringing in some flowers to enjoy at work. A store-bought bouquet or hand-picked flower will bring the beauty and scents of the outdoors in, and make your workday a bit brighter. You may find yourself treating yourself to flowers on a weekly basis!

12 Eat Your Favorite "Kid" Food

Eating like a kid is something you probably reserve for those late-night cravings when no one can catch you making a peanut butter and fluff sandwich with a side of animal crackers. There is nothing more comforting than the food we ate as children. Mac and cheese from a box, chicken fingers, and SpaghettiOs still make our mouths water, so just go for it. Tonight, plan to have all of your favorites for dinner.

13 Get a Reiki Treatment

Reiki (pronounced "ray-key") is a Japanese stress reduction and relaxation technique that also promotes healing. Each of us has a life energy force (sometimes referred to as *chi* or *ki*) that can sometimes become low or blocked. When this happens, we are more likely to feel stressed-out and sick. Reiki uses universal healing energy to remove these blockages and has the ability to heal mind, body, and spirit. A trained Reiki practitioner will lay their hands on or above you in various positions on your body to initiate the flow of healing energy. Practitioners can often feel where there is a blockage and may concentrate on a specific area longer than others. A normal session lasts about an hour. After a Reiki session, you will experience feelings of relaxation, peace, and well-being.

14 Go Apple Picking

When autumn approaches, a favorite activity is apple picking. Take the time to visit an orchard when the apples are ready (usually mid-September to mid-October). Searching for the perfect apple can be a real treat. Most orchards have a variety of apples like McIntosh, Cortland, Golden Delicious, and Granny Smith. The best part is taking them home to make a pie or apple crisp. Make this a family trip or go with a group of friends. If you decide to go alone, take the time to stop and breathe in the crisp, fall air and the delicious smell of fresh apples.

. . . .

15 *Learn How to Knit*

Knitting is no longer for little old ladies. According to Craft Yarn Council of America, "the number of women knitters in the U.S. age 25–35 increased 150 percent between 2002 and 2004." Although it is usually done alone, knitting has become a social activity. With popular books like *The Friday Night Knitting Club* and *The Knitting Circle* and countless blogs devoted to sharing patterns and techniques, knitting has re-emerged as a hot hobby. Knitting might seem difficult to learn, but with the right teacher or guide you'll pick it up in no time. Many people find it to be extremely relaxing and a great way to wind down at the end of a long day. You can let yourself get lost in the repetition of knit one, purl two. The best part is you can bring your work with you anywhere you go. It is satisfying to make something like a scarf or a winter hat and give it to a friend or family member, so go out and buy yourself a pair of needles and some beautiful, soft yarn that catches your eye. Join a local knitting club and meet new friends or stay home and relax—your new hobby will make you happy and stress free either way.

16 Buy Expensive Sheets for Your Bed

We spend one-third of our lives in bed sleeping. Don't you want that bed to be as comfortable as possible? Sure, sheets can be expensive, but you don't need to buy them that often, so make the investment. Take a trip to your favorite department store and splurge on a high thread count. The higher the thread count the softer the sheets will feel, and that's always a good thing. If you're really worried about the price, try finding some at a discount store. They often have a wide variety of expensive bedding items at cheaper prices.

17 Test Drive a Car You Can't Afford

There are some things you know you'll never be able to afford, unless by some divine miracle you win the lottery or become Hollywood's new sweetheart. One of those things is a ridiculously expensive car like a Lamborghini or a Ferrari. Who says you can't pretend though? Dress up in your Sunday best, head to the nearest luxury car dealership, and act like you can afford any of the cars in there. Tell the dealer you are the CEO of a *Fortune* 500 company just stopping in before your trip to the Caymans. Choose your favorite car and take it out for a spin; let yourself get lost in the fantasy. When you get back from your adventure, tell the dealer you're looking for something a bit more extravagant and walk out. You might only be able to afford a Toyota, but they need never know.

18 Have Breakfast for Dinner

Breakfast consists of some of the best foods ever created, but many of us only have time on the weekends to make an extravagant breakfast. Belgian waffles with whipped cream and strawberries, pancakes or French toast with butter and maple syrup, ham and cheese omelets with bacon or sausage are all great options for dinner. Even a simple bowl of cereal, bananas, and milk can be comforting after a stressful day. Make some of your favorites tonight, and don't forget the mimosas.

19 Join Paperback Swap

Hailed by O, the Oprah Magazine as "the best thing to come along since the public library," www.paperbackswap.com is a website where people can swap books with other members for free. You post books (they don't have to be paperback) that you don't want anymore. Each book you post earns you a credit. You can then search through the database to find books that you want. Paperback and hardcover books are only one credit. Audio books are two. If you want a book that hasn't been posted, you can add it to your wish list. When another member posts it, you will be notified and then you can request that they send it. The only money you have to pay is the postage for sending books. Postage is normally $2–$3. They also have chat rooms where you can talk with other members and recommend books to each other. This is a great way to clean out your bookcases, get new books for free, and meet some new people who share your love of reading.

20 Collect Shells at the Beach

One of the best activities to do at the beach is collect seashells. Grab a big bucket and go for a long walk on the shore. You will find many varieties of shells like iridescent mussel shells and scalloped shells. You might even find some other treasures like starfish, driftwood, sea glass, and stones that the waves and sand have polished. You can use the shells that you find as decoration in your house. Pile them onto a plate and place a large pillar candle in the middle that reminds you of the ocean. Or just keep them in a special box and add to them every year. These natural mementos will make you feel like digging your toes in the warm sand, even in the middle of winter.

21 *Forgive Someone*

Today, take the time to let someone know that you forgive them. This isn't always an easy task, but forgiving someone for hurting you is important for your mind and body. When you hold onto grudges, you carry unwanted stress and anger. If you can't say "I forgive you" in person, write a letter or just say it out loud to the universe. Find your own way to let it go. You will feel it in your heart when you do.

22 *Wash Each Other in the Shower*

Showering together can be practical as well as foreplay. You'll be saving water and driving each other crazy at the same time. Let the hot water relax you, then lather each other up with a moisturizing body wash. Clean each other from head to foot, giving light kisses as you go. Take turns washing each other's hair. A nice scalp rub can feel divine, especially when it's from the one you love. When you are squeaky clean, take it to the bedroom to finish your fun.

23 Restock Your Fruit Bowl

Take a trip to the grocery store and buy at least one piece of fruit for every day of the week. Try to get a variety of different fruits like apples, grapes, oranges, and bananas. Or you can try exotic fruits like mangos, papayas, kiwis, star fruit, and guava. A full fruit bowl isn't just good for you, it can be a pretty centerpiece as well. If you've never had a fruit bowl before, now is your chance to start eating fruit every day. If you fill it with your favorites, you'll be more likely to grab a piece than the bag of chips in your junk drawer.

24 Wear Fluffy Socks

A pair of very soft, fluffy socks can feel like heaven to sore feet. Tonight, give yourself a foot rub or ask your partner to give you one, using some peppermint-scented lotion. It will cool and moisturize your dry or cracked feet. Then put on a pair of your favorite fluffy socks. They can be made of chenille or angora, cashmere or soft cotton.

25 *Bake a Birthday Cake*

On our birthdays, most of us are lucky enough to be treated to our favorite kind of cake. But why wait all year to enjoy your favorite Funfetti or decadent red velvet? Bake a birthday cake and treat yourself and your family to the deliciousness of a cake without the awkwardness of singing "Happy Birthday." Or, go the whole nine yards and blow out the candles and make a wish. Your family might think you're crazy but all will be forgiven when you cut the cake!

26 *Have a Sleepover*

You probably haven't had friends sleep at your house since you were a teenager. Tonight, get a group of friends to stay over. Tell them to bring their sleeping bags and pillows. Stay up late watching scary movies, eating junk food, playing board games, and catching up on gossip. This time you won't have to worry about waking your parents up in the middle of the night.

27 Get a Tattoo

You know you've thought of getting a tattoo at some point in your life. Maybe you were out partying with friends and almost made a big mistake after a few too many drinks. Or perhaps you've just been putting it off because of your fear of needles. Tattoos are no longer reserved for sailors and prisoners. Everyone seems to have a Chinese symbol on their lower back or a ring of barbed wire around their bicep. You don't need to do it to be trendy, however. Think long and hard about something that is truly meaningful to you: your child's initials or a tribute to a loved one who has passed placed in a discreet spot. Get something tasteful that you won't regret in the morning.

28 Cut Down Your Own Christmas Tree

There is nothing nicer than the smell of a real Christmas tree filling your home during the holidays. Make this tradition extra special by going to a local Christmas tree farm and cutting it down yourself. Many tree farms let you pick out the tree that you want in the fall, tag it so everyone knows that it is yours, then cut it down in December. It might take a bit of strength to chop down the tree, but it will be well worth it. You'll know that it is fresh and meant just for you. You can even buy trees that you can replant in your yard. That way a tree doesn't have to die for the sake of decoration.

29 Take a Cooking Class with a Friend

It's always fun to learn a new skill, and learning how to cook can be a money saver as well. Why call for take-out when you can whip up a gourmet meal in no time? Sign up with a friend for a cooking class with your local adult education program or community college. Some schools offer different types of classes like baking and cake decorating or Italian cuisine. Many classes run for a short period, like a six-week program; if you're serious about cooking, you can sign up for a whole term. You'll be able to take home whatever you make, which will be a real treat for those you live with.

30 Buy a Star

For $50, you can own a piece of the heavens—your very own star. Check out www.starregistry.com to buy a unique gift or claim one for yourself. You even get to name it, perhaps honoring a loved one's memory by naming it after him or her. Once you purchase the star, the International Star Registry will send you a certificate with the name of your personalized star as well as a map that shows where it is in the night sky. This might seem like a scam, but it can be quite a romantic gift for someone you love.

31 Make Homemade Fruit Popsicles

Popsicles are a favorite summertime treat, but they are usually made with high-fructose corn syrup and water. Instead, make your own popsicles using 100 percent fruit juice. Fill an ice-cube tray with your favorite juice. Cover the tray with two or three layers of aluminum foil, and poke wooden sticks through the foil into each individual tray square (you can find sticks at your local craft store). Place the tray in the freezer and wait until they are fully frozen. In a few hours, you'll have a delicious snack that is good for you. Try to use exotic fruit juices like mango or guava. You can't always find these types of popsicles in the store, and if you serve them at a barbecue you'll definitely impress your friends. Enjoy this guiltless snack today!

32 *Cut Coupons*

You know those fliers you get every week in the mail? You normally throw them in the trash, right? Today, look through them and cut some coupons. You might find items you usually buy or haven't tried because they are too expensive. Coupons are practically free money, and in times like these, who can turn down free money? You can get some really great deals, and it only takes a few minutes of your day. Every little bit helps, and you'll feel better when you see your weekly grocery receipt.

33 *Have an '80s Movie Marathon*

Movie marathons are a great way to relax on the weekend, especially if it is raining or snowing and you are stuck in the house. Themed movie marathons are even better. Today, rent all of your '80s favorites like *Sixteen Candles*, *The Breakfast Club*, *Ferris Bueller's Day Off*, and *Back to the Future*. Have some friends over and dress up in '80s fashions. Break out the leg warmers and members-only jackets. If '80s movies aren't your style, have a Lord of the Rings marathon or a *Matrix* trilogy weekend.

34 *Get Your Tarot Cards Read*

If you've never had your cards read before, it can be a very enlightening experience. Ask friends or coworkers if they can recommend a reader. There are many different types of readers, and if someone has had a good experience they can lead you in the right direction. Stay away from places that advertise with neon-lit signs, and keep in mind that a serious reader won't look mystical. Go into the reading with an open mind and an open heart. If you close yourself off, the reader won't be able to give you information easily. Readers use different types of cards and put them in different positions. Not all readers read the same way, and they don't receive information the same way. The more open you are, the better reading you will have. Many people wonder how tarot can seem so accurate. One theory is like attracts like: If you are giving off a certain type of energy by thinking specific thoughts, you will be drawn to pick the cards that correspond with that energy. This works with your subconscious thoughts as well. Talented readers can also pick up on that energy and interpret it so it clarifies any problems or questions you might have. Be sure to ask the reader any questions you have about how it all works; they will be happy to share.

35 Buy Lingerie for No Reason

You normally buy sexy lingerie when you have a big date or if you know someone will be seeing it later that night. Today, buy something hot for no reason and wear it out. Sure, maybe nobody will see it, but you'll know it's there. Something as simple as a see-through thong or lace panties will make you feel sexy and will be your own little secret.

36 Buy Flowers for Every Room

Fresh-cut flowers for every room in your house will not only smell wonderful, but will make each room feel special. Choose daisies or sunflowers for the kitchen—bright welcoming flowers for the most popular room in your house. Long-stem roses for the bedroom will add a bit of romance and elegance. A small bouquet of lilacs in the bathroom will be simple yet beautiful and smell lovely. If it is autumn, a vase of hearty mums can be a gorgeous centerpiece for the dining room or coffee table in the living room. Choose your favorites, and if you can, pick wildflowers to save money. They will make you smile all year round.

37 Shower Until the Hot Water Runs Out

Sometimes the only way to wind down after a particularly stressful day is to take a long, hot shower. Don't worry about saving some hot water for someone else; enjoy it all yourself. Let the hot water wash your stress and anxiety away. Take your time doing your cleaning routine and be gentle with yourself. Sometimes it's nice to just stand there and do some deep breathing. It might take a long time for all the hot water to run out, so just enjoy your time alone.

38 Pamper Yourself During Pregnancy

When you're expecting a baby, life might feel like a whirlwind of doctor's appointments and blood tests peppered with some nausea, weight gain, and exhaustion. Take yourself out for a spa day or a prenatal yoga class. Or stay inside and make some homemade cookies. A hot cup of tea and some girl talk could be just the thing you need, so invite a girlfriend along. Once you have the baby, it will be more difficult to schedule time together, so take advantage now.

39 Build a Fort

Remember how fun it was to build an elaborate fort in the backyard or the living room when you were a kid? Relive those days, and gather all of your blankets and pillows to build your own getaway. Rearrange the furniture and drape the blankets over them to create an optimal fort. Lay the pillows on the floor so you can relax comfortably, and bring in some small lamps. This can be a nice area to read a book or start that novel you've always wanted to write. Don't worry about what's going on outside—the fort is your sanctuary for today.

40 Treasure Hunt on the Beach

You never know when you might find something valuable on the beach; people drop money and jewelry all of the time. Many coastlines hold the remnants of old sunken ships from the past, and their treasure often washes up on the beach years later. A number of beaches along the Florida coast, like Vero Beach, are known for having treasure wash ashore from Spanish fleets that sank off the coast. All you need is a good metal detector to claim some of the gold and treasure—you can get a decent one for under $100. Take your time walking up and down the beach; you never know what you might find.

41 Buy Yourself a Christmas Present

With the hustle and bustle of the holidays, we often forget to do something nice for ourselves. While you are out shopping for friends and family, pick out a gift just for you. Maybe it's a new outfit for a holiday party or a new winter coat. You could also splurge on something extravagant that you wouldn't want to ask someone to buy for you. Wrap up the present and wait until Christmas morning to open it. You know there will be one present under the tree that you really like.

42 Cook Sunday Dinner for Your Family

Sunday dinner is a tradition upheld by many families. Invite some family over for a late-afternoon meal. It doesn't have to be a fancy affair; Sunday dinner is usually casual. The most important thing is the food and the company. Make lasagna or a chicken dinner with all of the trimmings. You can feed a lot of people and you won't have to spend all day cooking. Have someone else bring the dessert. Take this time to enjoy each other and laugh. It is a nice tradition to follow before the beginning of the workweek.

43 Visit the Zoo

The zoo can be a great place to relax and enjoy nature. This might be the only place you will ever see lions or penguins up close. Go to your local zoo today. Many libraries offer discount tickets or coupons to local attractions—check with yours to see if you can get a discount for the zoo. Spending the day appreciating these incredible creatures will help you put things into perspective. Don't skip the informative signs throughout the zoo—read as many as you can so you walk away with something you never knew before about a species.

44 Make a Recipe from Your Favorite Cooking Show

Thanks to the Food Network, cooking shows are more popular than ever. With such a wide variety of cooking shows, you're sure to find a recipe you'll love. Spend the day learning how to cook from the pros. When you find a dish you'd really like to try, write it down and head over to the grocery store. Invite some friends over to try your creation or include them in your cooking adventure. It will be fun and delicious.

45 Buy a Lottery Ticket

Everyone dreams of winning the lottery, but you can't win if you don't play. So, pick up a few scratch tickets on your way home from work or choose a few special numbers for a lotto ticket. Keno can also be fun and is found in many sports bars and convenience stores. Just don't end up like the folks that sit there all day trying to figure out a pattern. You can also host a scratch-ticket party. Have everyone pitch in $20 and go pick up all the scratch-offs you can get. Agree to split the profits should you win a substantial prize. You might lose all of your money in the first round, but you'll have fun doing it.

46 Go to the Movie Theater Alone

You might pity those people you see sitting alone at the movie theater, but they're probably really enjoying themselves. You don't need another person to go with you. It's not like you can talk during the movie. If you go alone, you can see any movie you want, even ones you wouldn't want anyone to know you saw. It's nice to be alone in a dark theater eating all the popcorn and Goobers you want. Look up an early matinee that you might be interested in. You'll pay a cheaper price and you'll probably have the theater all to yourself. Enjoy your time alone.

47 Tell Someone You Love Them

This can be either easy or hard, depending on if you've ever told that person you love them before. Saying it out loud can make you and the other person feel amazing, so it's worth it. Maybe you've been waiting to tell your new boyfriend or girlfriend your true feelings. Maybe you haven't told your mom or dad you love them in a while. If you were never particularly close enough to your brother or sister to say the "L" word regularly, do it today. There is no time like the present and everyone needs to hear "I love you." Say it loud and proud.

48 Have a Sex-Toy Party

If you have always wanted to experiment with sex toys but have been too afraid to walk into a sex shop, a sex-toy party is perfect for you. Research some sex-toy company consultants like Athena's or Passion Parties. Invite all of your girlfriends and serve some light appetizers and cocktails. The consultant will show you a variety of lubricants, vibrators, and novelties like handcuffs and whips. You might learn something you never knew before. As the host, you will get a percentage of the total price of your party to spend on toys of your choice. The more your friends spend, the more free stuff you get.

49 Rearrange Your Bedroom

Having your bed in the same place all of the time can get a little boring. Mix it up and rearrange your whole bedroom today. Try to place your bed near a window so you can wake up in the sun. You can also get fresh air when the weather is nice. If you have a TV in your bedroom, try to get rid of it. Couples who have a television in the bedroom have sex half as much as those who don't. While you're moving furniture around, take the time to vacuum and dust to get all of the allergens out of your room—you don't want to breathe that in all night. These small changes can make a big difference.

50 Moisturize with Warm Lotion

Getting out of hot shower into a cold bathroom can feel quite unpleasant. Why give yourself more goose bumps with cold lotion? Heat the lotion up ahead of time and you'll be in for a delightful treat. You don't need to use the oven or microwave to do this, just keep the bottle of lotion near or on your radiator or heating vent during the winter. The warm lotion will feel luxurious on your body.

51 *Jazz Up Your Leftovers*

These days, everyone is looking to save a dollar. With grocery bills continuing to climb, an easy way to do this is to cut down on wasted food by eating your leftovers. But by day two of roasted chicken and vegetables, the thought of eating the same meal yet again can be unappealing. Give new life to your meals by jazzing up your leftovers. Try adding different spices, herbs, or sauces and that chicken and vegetables becomes sizzling fajitas. Those leftover hamburger patties can be transformed to a cheesy lasagna. You'll still eat your leftovers, but your palate will be pleased with the variety!

52 *Camp Out in the Backyard*

Break out the tent, flashlights, and s'mores! If you love to camp but can't get away for the weekend, you can sleep under the stars without being far from home. If you've never camped before, this can be a primer. A camp out in the backyard can be just as fun as in the woods . . . and you can still use your own toilet. Set up your tent and bring all of your warm blankets and pillows. If you bring out your laptop or portable DVD player, you can watch scary movies all night. No camp out would be complete without s'mores, so build a fire pit in your backyard or take the easy way out and make them in the house.

53 Dig for Gemstones

Whether it's the opal mines in Nevada or the ruby mines of North Carolina, many gemstone mines allow you to dig your own for a reasonable price. Do some research online to find a gemstone mine in your area or plan a weekend getaway. You will get a bucket and a shovel so you can collect as much dirt from the mine as possible. Then you use a sifter to shake the dirt away from the gems. You might find small ones or you might find larger pieces. Whatever you find is yours to keep, and some walk away with very valuable gemstones. This can turn into an addictive hobby. Bring your family or friends for a day of fun.

54 Decorate Your Cubicle or Office for the Holidays

If you are like the majority of Americans who work too much, you probably spend more time at the office than in your own home. Decorate your work space for the holidays or just for the season. Make sure your company doesn't have any rules about decorations that might conflict with your festive cheer. String Christmas or Hanukkah lights, hang spooky bats for Halloween, get some stuffed turkeys for your desk. Whatever time of year it is, find a way to make your office or cubicle festive. It will make it a place you want to be . . . even during the holidays.

55 Have an Ice Cream Social

Who doesn't like ice cream sundaes? They are always a crowd pleaser. Have some friends over for an old-fashioned ice cream social. Provide a few different flavors of ice cream and have your friends bring their favorite topping like nuts, sprinkles, cherries, or hot fudge. Don't forget the whipped cream. You can award a prize for the best sundae, which will give you an excuse to try them all. You can also make ice cream floats and shakes or buy an ice cream cake. This is a great idea for a summertime party.

56 Lie Out Under the Stars

Sometimes all it takes is lying down in the grass and looking up at the infinite sky to remind you that we are a small piece of this incredible universe. It is extremely beneficial to take time to appreciate the beauty of what lies beyond us and help put our daily stress into perspective. Taking this time out will help relax your mind and inspire you to do big things! Make sure to turn off those backyard sensor lights that will go off with a passing wind!

57 Have Dessert for Dinner

Have you ever gone to a restaurant just to get the dessert, but by the time you have finished your entrée you are too stuffed for that sweetness? Well, try switching things up—treat yourself to your favorite dessert for the first course and don't leave room for dinner! This simple reward can help put that much-needed smile on your face at the end of a long day.

58 Create a Budget

This may come as a complete shock, but many people go their whole lives without creating a formal budget for themselves. It may seem tedious at first, but it is truly rewarding in the long run. Putting your expenses in writing can help you plan for that future vacation or help you pay off that burdensome debt from last Christmas. Whatever the reason may be, sit down with a pen and paper or at the computer and organize your monthly income and expenditures to take a closer look at where your money is going. Seeing your money in a more organized way can help you plan for the future and avoid those unsettling "money crunch" moments.

59 *Spend the Day in Bed*

How many mornings do you wake up before work and just want to lie in bed all day? Why not? Take a day off from work and don't leave bed all day. If need be, grab your laptop and work from the comfort of your pillows and duvet. If taking a day off is impossible, then on Saturday or Sunday, when you should be taking care of the weekend chores, enjoy your meals and a few good movies from your sleeping sanctuary. Although you may get restless and want to get up and clean those dirty dishes, fight the temptation and try to allow your body to relax and enjoy some R&R. If you have to, use a "Do Not Disturb" sign on the door to keep out any unwanted guests.

60 *Apologize to Someone*

It is one of the hardest and most challenging things to do. By holding in those guilty or regretful thoughts, your mind and soul are weighed down by the extra baggage that prohibits you from living life to its fullest. But admitting you are wrong and apologizing to someone will not only make them feel better, it will heal the past. Think of apologizing to someone as cleaning out that dirty attic that is getting dark and cluttered. If you are not the best with words, a handwritten note is the way to go.

61 Spend the Day Naked

Less is more. Enjoy a day in your own skin and only that. Choose a day when you don't need to leave the house to enjoy your birthday suit all day without any interruptions. Allowing yourself to be free will make you feel sexy. Sometimes the possibility of someone seeing you through the window will keep you giddy all day. Naked time can arouse your lover or yourself and help liven up a dull night. Be mindful of sharp edges and hot appliances!

62 Buy New Bath Towels

It is one of the easiest ways to start your morning off right. After stepping out of the hot shower, you deserve to wrap yourself in a nice, soft towel to dry off and keep you toasty. Go out today and splurge on a few expensive towels that you can use every day or save for those pampering moments. If you have any towels that have a hole or snags or are just plain ugly, throw them out! You deserve better! Always remember to save one of the nice ones as a guest towel.

63 Make an Appointment for a Physical

The most important indulgence in life is to take care of your body. It is the only one you have, and you must take it for a yearly tune-up to ensure everything is working properly. A great deal of people are nervous about doctors and therefore skip these crucial appointments; however, they should be looked at as a "you" moment. If you are uncomfortable with your doctor, get a new one. You should feel 100 percent in control and completely comfortable with your doctor. You work hard for those benefits, and it is your right and responsibility to make sure your "temple" is well taken care of.

64 Go Caroling

During the hustle of the holiday season, it can be easy to lose your spirit. The next time you find yourself overwhelmed by the to-do lists and obligations that come along with Christmas and Hanukkah, print a few sets of lyrics to popular holiday songs and get a few friends or family members to join you in a spirited evening of caroling. You'll bring smiles to your neighbors' faces and be reinvigorated with the holiday spirit you've been missing.

65 Take a Trip to Walt Disney World

Yes, it truly is the "happiest place on earth," and while you might think you need to be under the age of twelve to really enjoy Mickey's home, think again. There are plenty of "adult" activities like golf and the annual Food and Wine Festival at Epcot, but you won't be able to resist feeling like a kid when you look down Main Street, U.S.A, in the Magic Kingdom and see Cinderella Castle in all its glory. The four parks—Magic Kingdom, Epcot, Disney's Hollywood Studios, and Animal Kingdom—offer something no other theme parks can: the chance to be a kid again. Your eyes open wide with wonder, you get butterflies in your stomach waiting in line for a ride, you scream your guts out on Space Mountain and The Tower of Terror. This is the one place you can let go and forget about your adult responsibilities. So grab a Mickey bar or a famous Dole Whip, and get in line to ride Pirates of the Caribbean for the millionth time. Walt Disney World is magical for a reason, so book your trip today!

66 Take a Cheap Flight on a Whim

Feeling like you need to change things up a little and add some spontaneity to your life? Check your preferred airline's website and see what the cheapest flight is for that upcoming weekend. Maybe it is only a two- or three-day getaway, but leaving the day-to-day monotony behind and taking an exciting last-minute trip will remind you why you work those grueling hours in the first place. Taking some time away can help you put your life back into perspective and help remind you of what is important in life. The spontaneity of the trip will also lessen the stress leading up to the getaway. It is said that the best time to purchase inexpensive airline tickets is Wednesday evening.

67 *Send Holiday Cards*

Remember the way you feel when you receive that first holiday card in the mail? It takes a few minutes and a few dollars to send them out, but it truly shows your loved ones how grateful you are that they're in your life. In these difficult economic times, if sending a gift is not possible, a card with a personal greeting inside can go a long way. The best time to purchase holiday cards is right after the holidays in early January, when they are all at least 50 percent off. Just don't forget you have them when the time comes. Spread that holiday cheer!

68 Dress Up for Your Favorite Awards Show

Whether it be the Oscars or the Grammy Awards, invite your friends over to enjoy the show with you. It must be required that they dress up as if they were attending the award show. As an incentive to have them come dressed up, announce that there will be an award given out to the best dressed for the evening. Make sure to have the appropriate food and beverages for the event, including champagne for a toast. You may want to consider rolling out a red carpet and having another friend take photos of those arriving to the party to help create the mood.

69 Go Camping

Real camping! Try to avoid the modern technologies and your everyday luxuries. Find a national park where running water and electricity are not provided and plan a weekend away from the noise of your everyday life. Including a hike into the trip can bring some necessary exercise to the relaxing getaway. Make sure to check with your local forest department about any important warnings including rough terrain or animals. Unfortunately, in today's world, it wouldn't be smart to leave your cell phone behind; however, turn it off and leave the battery fully charged in case of an emergency. All you iPhone lovers—turn them off! There was once a day when e-mail did not exist and the world continued. . . .

70 *Set Up a Taco Bar*

Good Mexican food is hard to come by and who doesn't love tacos, guacamole, and margaritas? Tonight set up a taco bar in your kitchen. Lay out all of the fixings like seasoned meat, shredded lettuce, diced tomatoes, spicy cheese, and sour cream. Serve both hard and soft shells and don't forget the salsa. A taco bar is definitely more fun with friends so invite them over for a fiesta!

71 *Get a Copy of Your Credit Report*

You can never be too careful with your money, and especially your credit report. Your report is what every financial institution looks at before those big, important expenses like a home, car, or student loan. You can receive a free yearly credit report from *www.freecreditreport.com*. It will make you feel better knowing your credit is in order and there are no mistakes or fraud sitting next to your name. If there are any problems, you can have them fixed or work on bettering your score so you are ready in the future for those exciting purchases.

72 People Watch

Go to your local park, mall, or town center and take a seat. Take some time to observe what humans do and say—it will definitely make you laugh! Try to listen to the conversations as people walk by. You will find great pleasure in hearing the snippets of peoples' lives, and even realize that we are all alike in many ways. You may find your single self rating those other singles as potential mates or just guessing what kind of underwear they are wearing. Some of the best things to see occur when people think no one is watching. You thought mature adults don't pick their noses? Think again!

73 Meditate Before Bed

After a long day, your body, soul, and mind need a break before falling asleep. It is important to take some quiet time before putting yourself to bed to help calm all your senses and prepare for a good night's sleep. Light a candle, lie down, close your eyes, and think about absolutely nothing. Focus on relaxing each part of your body from your toes to your head. Think of each muscle group letting go of all the tension and releasing the day's stress. You may want to end your meditation with a quick prayer in thanks for that day and hopes for the next one.

· ·

74 Swim Naked

There is something about swimming naked that feels wonderful and immediately puts a smile on your face. It is the pleasure of doing something "wrong," but knowing it is really not that bad. For those risk-takers, taking a naked swim in the ocean in broad daylight can be fun, but remember it is illegal unless at a clothing-optional beach. Some prefer a naked night swim in their backyard pool. It feels just as dangerous, but in the end you are in the comforts of your own property. Swimming naked with your lover can be very erotic, but stick to pool or lake water as opposed to the ocean when considering having some "fun." The sand in the salt water can be quite uncomfortable when "snuggling" up with your partner.

75 Decorate for the Holidays

Get into the holiday spirit and decorate your home. Whether it's Halloween, the Fourth of July, or Christmas, it will constantly remind you of the holiday and keep you in the spirit. Purchase a few clear, plastic boxes to store each holiday's decorations. It is helpful to label each box with the holiday so it is easily accessible when it comes time to decorate. Decorating your home is a great activity to do with your partner or child. The memories of decorating will be just as memorable as the decorations themselves.

76 Get Your Teeth Cleaned

Getting your teeth cleaned may seem anything but blissful, but taking care of your teeth is so important. We all seem to put off the dentist appointment for anything that comes up, but it should be one of our top priorities. Not only are teeth part of your body, but they are essential to digesting food and something everyone sees in every picture—your smile. It can become very costly as you get older if you decide to let your teeth go and not get them cleaned every six months. To cut down on those bills and the worry of a potential problem, remember to take a few minutes out of every day and brush your teeth at least three times and floss.

77 Ask Your Lover to Spoil You

What guy or girl could resist when that special someone asks to be spoiled in the bedroom? Set the mood by lighting some candles and wearing something sexy, then let your partner know it's time to show you how much he or she cares. You'll both be treated on this special night!

78 Make a Snowman

The first snowfall of winter can be a beautiful sight. Celebrate the snow by making a snowman on your front lawn or in a park. Wait until you have the first big snowstorm. There will be a lot to work with, and you want to make sure it's that good snowman-making snow—nice and dense and easy to roll. Remember a few lumps of coal or rocks for the eyes and mouth and a carrot for the nose. Use an old hat and scarf to give him more personality. Sticks and gloves can be used for arms and hands. Be creative and have fun.

79 *Buy Yourself a Diamond*

We usually wait for someone to give us diamonds. Either we're waiting for an engagement ring or special earrings on our birthday. You can't wait forever, and you deserve it! Pick out a beautiful diamond for yourself. It could be a simple set of studs or a floating diamond necklace. Maybe you want to go all the way and buy a diamond ring; you know you'll be with yourself forever, so why not.

80 *See Fireworks on the Fourth of July*

Get out there and celebrate this great country with your friends and family! In almost every town there is some type of celebration that ends with a fireworks display. Find your nearest park, beach, or even parking lot and grab a blanket and a bottle of wine to enjoy the colors in the sky! Make this a tradition with a group of friends or family to meet at the same place every year so you can enjoy some quality time with the people you love. If for some reason you can't make it to an outside location, tune into one of the major networks and watch them from the comforts of home. Don't forget to wear red, white, and blue!

81 Have a Jewelry-Swap Party

We all have jewelry we don't wear anymore. Normally, we stick it in a box in a drawer, never to be seen again . . . though we refuse to throw it out. Chances are your girlfriends do the same thing, so now is the perfect time to have a jewelry-swap party. Have your friends bring their old necklaces, bracelets, earrings, and pins and display everything on a table. People can choose what they want or make a fair trade. This is a good way to clean out the drawers and get some new stuff for free.

82 Watch the Sunrise and Sunset in One Day

Sunrises and sunsets are two beautiful experiences that occur every day. Today, wake up early, grab a cup of coffee, and find the perfect view so you can catch the sunrise. It will energize you for the day. The sunset will have a totally different feel, but will be just as gorgeous. We don't often take the time to notice these two actions, but they are there every day for us to experience.

83 Celebrate with Champagne

Even if you don't have a special occasion like an anniversary or birthday to celebrate, break out a good bottle of bubbly and a fancy champagne flute. To make it even more special, put a strawberry in the drink. You can do this by yourself or with a loved one. Give a toast to honor something you are proud of or happy about today. A little sense of occasion on an otherwise boring night will make you feel special. Don't forget that just waking up in the morning is a reason to celebrate.

84 Keep a Journal for a Year

Time goes by so fast that we often forget to stop and realize what we've accomplished or taken part in during the year. Starting today, keep a journal and write in it every day for a year. At the end of the year, you'll be amazed at what you did, how you felt, and what you got through. This is a great way to reflect on the past but also make plans for the future. You'll learn from your mistakes as well as remember the great times you had. In ten years, you can pull out that journal and have a laugh. You'll likely find that what you thought was important wasn't, and you'll see how much you've changed.

85 *Enjoy a Day of Silence*

Set aside a day when you have nothing planned to enjoy a day of complete silence. Let your family and loved ones know that you will not be picking up the phone or answering any e-mails. This will cut down on the angry voice mails and texts that you will receive. If needed, create a password for others, like three phone calls in a row, that could signal an emergency. This day should not include television, music or any other "noisy" distractions. Silence can help us do some soul-searching or simply allow us to pay attention to the amount of vocalizing we do every day. Curl up on the couch with a good book or magazine and let those vocal cords take a nice rest.

86 *Go to an Open House for Your Dream Home*

Whether it is a random discovery while taking a morning walk or something you see in your local real estate guide, go to the open house of a home you definitely can't afford. It may be your dream home, but the real estate agent doesn't need to know that. Walk in like you could own the place tomorrow and enjoy the daydream. This is a great way to keep your goals set high and to remind yourself why you work so hard every day. You may also see some ideas that you can use in your current home for a much lower price. End the walk-through by telling the agent that, "it is just too small for our needs" and walk out with a smile.

87 Go to a Nude Beach

There are clothing-optional beaches all over the world. It may seem weird for the first couple of minutes, but once you are there for a while, it becomes awkwardly normal. We forget that countries around the world don't view nudity in the way America does. Nude beaches in some parts of Europe are practically standard. There is no shame in it and it has nothing to do with sex. It's about being free in a natural environment, and avoiding tan lines. If you think you will be too embarrassed to try this with a friend or partner, go alone for the first time. Go at your own pace, but remember that your body is beautiful no matter what size or shape and you should be proud of it. Don't forget the 50 SPF for those places where the sun normally doesn't shine.

88 Clean Out Your Refrigerator

You might be scared of what is living in your fridge. Perhaps you forgot about that leftover lasagna that got pushed to the back and hasn't been seen for two months. Maybe your fruit drawer is holding onto a pineapple from last summer that now looks unrecognizable. Whatever the case may be, it's time to clean out the refrigerator. Throw away the seven types of mustard you've accumulated and the half-empty bottles of salad dressing. The key here is if you didn't even know that you had it, it's time to get rid of it. This task isn't just about clearing out old food, though—you'll need to wash the inside with hot water and soap. Make it look like new. Think of the number of times you open your fridge in a single day. You want to see it shine, right? You'll be happy when it's all over.

89 *Take a Daily Vitamin*

Many people don't get the vital nutrients they need from food alone. Taking a daily vitamin can assist you in living a long and healthy life. Vitamins help you release energy from the food you eat and build strong bones and tissue. Vitamins can be expensive, but they are a small price to pay when you think of how it is helping your body stay in tip-top shape. Consult with your doctor on what vitamin will be the best for your body and if it might interfere with any medication you are currently taking. Women especially need calcium, while men greatly benefit from selenium.

90 Go One for You, One for Me

Many of us hold on to clothes that we haven't worn in years. If you no longer fit into something or you just don't like it anymore, let it go. Grab a bag and organize everything by clothing type and find the nearest charity where you can donate, like the Salvation Army. Then, treat yourself to something new—a shirt, suit, or dress that fits you well can make you feel great about yourself, and you can feel good about giving to someone in need.

91 Make Marshmallow and Rice Cereal Squares

No matter how old you are, you probably have fond memories of this classic after-school snack. If you had little patience, like most children, you probably ate them directly from the bowl with a spoon. You'll need the following ingredients:

3 tablespoons butter or margarine
1 (10-ounce) package marshmallows or 4 cups mini marshmallows
6 cups rice cereal

Melt the butter or margarine in a saucepan. Add the marshmallows to the melted butter and stir until they are completely melted. Remove pan from heat and stir in the rice cereal. Make sure all of the cereal is coated with the marshmallow and butter mixture. Pour into a 13" × 9" pan and spread evenly. When it cools, cut into squares. If you're feeling creative, add some chocolate or peanut butter chips to the mix. Make up your own recipe and bring them to work to share; your coworkers will love them.

92 Spend the Day at a Water Park

On a hot summer day, a water park can be heaven. A trip down the lazy river or an exhilarating ride down a water slide will cool you off in no time. If it's a particularly hot day, you might have to wait in long lines, but it will be worth it. Bring a friend so you can ride in an inner tube for two. Many water park rides have become more sophisticated than just a wave pool; some have designed water slides that feel like roller coasters. You're in for a treat.

93 Start Holiday Shopping in the Summer

It is never too early to start holiday shopping! It is understandable that you may not feel encouraged to shop in the summer, but you may find some great deals. Shopping early will give you the needed time to choose the perfect gift as opposed to waiting until the mad rush and picking something that is not as thoughtful for that special someone. Most importantly, shopping early will eliminate the added stress of crowded stores and large credit card bills. By planning ahead and spreading out the costs for holiday shopping, you will allow yourself to enjoy the holidays and not dread each day while standing in line at the crowded department stores.

94 Have a Traditional Summer Cookout

Fire up the barbecue and break out the badminton set—cookouts are a must during the summer. Invite some friends and family over for a traditional all-American cookout. That means hot dogs, hamburgers, barbecued chicken, potato salad, and beer. Bring a television outside so you can watch the baseball game if it's on or listen to the game on the radio. If the party runs into the night, set up a small fire in the backyard and make s'mores. Celebrate the season with good food and friends.

95 Dance in the Rain

Why do we always try to avoid those moments when Mother Nature drops some water on us? Next time it rains on one of those hot summer days, run outside and get wet! Don't be afraid to look like a fool. If Gene Kelly can look cool doing it, so can you. If you are embarrassed to have your neighbors see you, find that spot in your backyard where no one can see you and dance away. If you have a stereo system outside that is under cover, blast your favorite song so you can truly enjoy the moment.

96 Have an Exotic Meal for Dinner

We all get caught up in the daily routines of life and forget to try different foods. For dinner tonight, make something you have never eaten before or go out to dinner and try a new dish. Go beyond your comfort level and eat something from a foreign culture that would normally scare you. Be mindful to order a smaller portion, just in case you don't like it. In the end, you may discover that this type of food is not for you, but at least you can say you tried it. As the old saying says: You don't know until you've tried it.

97 Clean Your Desk Before Leaving Work

Get yourself ready for the next workday by cleaning up your work space before leaving. It may seem very simple, however, allowing the remnants of today's work to spill over to tomorrow can leave you feeling very unorganized and prohibit you from starting tomorrow with a fresh attitude. It will help create a priority to-do list for the next day. By taking a few minutes at the end of the day, you can drastically change tomorrow's workday.

98 Stay at a Bed and Breakfast

Plan a weekend away with your close friend or partner and stay at a comfy bed and breakfast. They are usually much more personable than major hotel chains and will often offer a complementary afternoon tea and refreshments or continental breakfast. It is best to plan a B&B getaway during those cold winter months when you can snuggle up next to the main living room's fireplace. If you are planning a romantic getaway, you may want to check into the "adult only" locations so you can be free of any noisy distractions.

99 Create a Goal Board

We all have a lot of goals and aspirations in life, but seeing them everyday reminds us to continue to reach for them in our everyday tasks. Use a corkboard or dry erase board and draw or cut out pictures or phrases that represent the ultimate job you want or that dream home you have been saving for. Make sure to hang this board in your home where you will see it every morning before you start your day. Whatever the goal may be, the visual daily reminder will help you focus your energy and get your creative juices flowing every time you see the board.

100 Kiss Passionately Before You Leave for Work

If you've been with your partner for a long time, you probably don't kiss like you used to . . . unless you're gearing up to have sex. Before you leave for work, kiss him like it's your last kiss. Kiss him passionately for more than ten seconds. It will give you that burst of energy you need before you walk out the door and start your day. It will also remind you to finish where you left off when you come home. A great kiss can make your day, so start it off right.

101 *Have Your House Blessed*

Before moving into a new place is the best time for a house blessing, but it will still work if you've lived there a while. Depending on your religion, you can have a priest or member of clergy come to your home or you can even try it yourself. Get some sage to burn as you walk around the house and through every room. Burning sage cleanses the room of any negative energy. You can then go room to room and say a prayer or just wish for happiness and peace while you live in the house.

102 *Get a Hot Stone Massage*

If you've never had a hot stone massage, you are in for a one-of-a-kind experience. The stones are used in two different ways during the massage. One way is by providing heat to areas of the body to make the muscles relax and increase blood flow to speed up healing. They are usually placed along the length of the spine or along the chakra centers of your body. A towel will be between you and the stones, so don't worry about being burned. Another way the stones are used is as tools for deep-tissue massage. Your massage therapist will cover the warm, smooth stones in oil and rub them on your body using long strokes in the area she is working on. This is an unbelievable sensation and one you will truly enjoy. If you are used to traditional Swedish massage, try this version instead.

103 *Make a Relaxing Playlist*

Compile twelve to fifteen songs that make you say, "ahhhhh." Whether it's classical or contemporary, instrumental or vocal-based, make sure each song puts you in a relaxed headspace. The next time you catch your blood pressure rising, put the playlist on in your car or pop in your ear buds and let the tranquil music soothe you.

104 *Play on a Swing*

If you haven't done this since your days on the playground at recess, get out there and swing! We liked swinging as a kid because it made us feel free as a bird. We would pump our little legs and try to swing higher than our friends. You probably even had a contest to see who could jump the farthest off the swing. A few minutes on a swing at the local playground will make you feel carefree again. Try to go when you have the park to yourself so you can really let loose. Let your head hang back as you enjoy the rush of wind hitting your face.

105 Ride a Roller Coaster

When you need that thrill to take the edge off, but still want to feel somewhat safe, take a ride on a roller coaster. You can go for the highest and fastest one at the park or jump on one of the old, wooden ones. It may be your first ride since you were a child, but just as you hit that first drop all the memories will come rushing back. Try not to eat a big meal before you ride, as it could cause you to lose your lunch! As of 2008, the world's fastest and tallest coaster—Kingda Ka—is right here in the United States, in Jackson, New Jersey, at Six Flags. Remember to keep any loose items in your pockets!

106 Eat a Boiled Dinner on St. Patrick's Day

Corned beef, cabbage, carrots, and potatoes, also called New England boiled dinner, is the traditional Irish-American St. Patty's meal. This is a very simple and cheap meal to prepare, and if you aren't Irish you can still enjoy it. If you live in New England, you likely know someone who celebrates the holiday, so ask them to come over for dinner. Top it off with some Irish soda bread and a Guinness and you are on your way to a festive and cheerful St. Patrick's Day feast.

107 *Have a Series Finale Party*

Is your favorite television show ending? Why not celebrate with your friends who will also mourn the show's end. Ask each person to bring a snack or drink that somehow connects to the show. Try creating a trivia game about the series that you can play after the finale to help cheer everyone up. The great news is that your show will probably be out on DVD within six months of the finale, so you can enjoy it over and over again.

108 *Go to an Outdoor Concert*

Attending a live music event is almost always an exhilarating experience. When you add the element of the outdoors it seems to elevate the energy of the crowd. Whether it is a cool, starry night or hot, summer day, the interaction of the loud music, roaring crowds, and nature all around will make for an enjoyable event. Make sure to invite your friends, as concerts are always best to experience with a group. If the event is during the summer, plan on arriving early and having a barbecue in the parking lot.

109 Eat Brownies for Breakfast

Go ahead, do it . . . no one is watching! It may not be the healthiest part of your balanced breakfast; however, it will be well worth it. The simple fact that it is against the rules may give you that energy boost you need. If you feel completely awful, cut up some strawberries to go along with the brownie. Always remember to treat yourself when you are having a stressful day. Sometimes it is the only way to pull you out of the dark hole you have sunk into. Be mindful of just how much sweetness you indulge in, as you may have a tough afternoon with an aching tummy!

110 Keep a Food and Exercise Journal

Start to keep track of everything you eat and all the exercise you take part in so you can monitor your work. Seeing what you eat every day can help you change your bad habits. Sometimes, just having to write down everything you eat will make you think twice about grabbing that bag of chips. It can also help you see where to add more healthy options such as an afternoon veggie snack instead of a candy bar. It is helpful to visualize your exercise regimen as well. You can create a schedule based on what muscle groups you want to focus on or simply how many miles you ran or walked that week. Make sure to track your progress so you can continue to motivate yourself.

111 Take a Nap

If your last nap was twenty to thirty years ago, take some time out today for a quick nap. A quick thirty-minute mid-day nap has been proven to lessen stress, increase learning, and improve health. This may be hard if you are at work, but even closing your eyes for five minutes in your office is proven to relieve stress and give you a boost of energy. Those few moments will help you decompress and give your body the needed break it deserves. Be careful of napping for more than an hour, as you may have a hard time falling asleep that evening.

112 Learn about Another Religion

There are many religions in the world, but all seem to serve the same purpose. They offer comfort in times of need, answer important questions like "Where do we go when we die?"

and offer us basic guidelines on how we should live our lives. Take some time to explore a religion whose history you aren't familiar with. You might be firm in your beliefs, but studying a different religion might open your mind to new ideas.

113 Get a Brazilian Wax

This might not be something you ever thought you would do, but it is quickly gaining popularity. A Brazilian wax, also known as a Hollywood wax, removes all of your pubic hair . . . all of it; not even a landing strip left. You should try everything once, so call up your favorite esthetician and go all the way. Your man will be completely surprised and most likely very turned on. After you get over the initial pain of the wax, you're sure to enjoy the clean and smooth feeling of being hairless. If you're too afraid to have someone wax you, buy a home wax kit or just go the old-fashioned route and shave it all off.

114 Repaint Your Bedroom

A simple coat of paint can do wonders to an otherwise plain room. If your bedroom needs a makeover, head down to your local hardware store and pick up a few cans of paint. Pick a color that reflects how you want your bedroom to feel. Paint it deep red to promote love and passion or light blue if you want a relaxing sanctuary. Stay away from really vibrant colors like bright pink or yellow, as they might make it hard to sleep! This is a quick and easy do-it-yourself job that will add value to your home for a low price.

115 *Get a Manicure*

Getting your nails cleaned and polished is a simple luxury that can be enjoyed by both men and women. A manicure is relatively inexpensive (normally $10–$12), but can get a bit pricey if you want acrylic nails or an elaborate paint job. The manicurist will soak your hands in a warm water bath until the cuticles are softened. They will then clip and clean around and under your nails. Usually, you are treated to a hand massage as well. You can then pick your color of polish or you can a pay a little bit more for a classic French manicure. Either way, you'll walk out with beautiful hands and nails.

116 *Go Wild at the Free Sample Table*

The next time you're shopping and there are free samples, quiet that voice in your head that tells you to move on after one sample. Why not go back for seconds or thirds? Most people giving away free samples won't mind if you treat yourself to an extra ramekin of chips and salsa or another sip of wine at the liquor store. The samples are meant to be taken, and you can return the favor by purchasing the item that you've enjoyed.

117 Jump in a Pile of Autumn Leaves

As children, jumping in a pile of leaves was one of the great things about fall. As adults, we see the leaves as a burden. Raking leaves is just another chore added to our busy schedule. The next time you rake your backyard and make a large pile of leaves, dive right into it before putting leaves in the bag. Roll around in the crunchy leaves and breathe in the smell of autumn. Remember to enjoy the red, orange, and gold colors of the season.

118 Gamble at a Casino

Even if you are not the gambling type, take out a specific amount of money that you are allowed to gamble with that day. Once you run out, the gambling must end. If you are lucky, you may win enough to have dinner on the casino and leave with your original amount. If you plan on spending a smaller amount, the slot machines can always be fun, and the drinks are still free. Don't underestimate the penny machines; you never know when you could strike the jackpot!

. . . .

119 Make a New Year's Resolution

Make a resolution this year and stick to it. It may be helpful to create your resolution list a few weeks before the first of the year to help you prepare. If committing to a few things is too stressful, focus all your energy on one important goal. If you plan to quit smoking or start a new exercise schedule, spend the few weeks leading up to New Year's doing your research and creating a realistic strategy to help you succeed. Create a timeline of the weeks and months after New Year's where you schedule rewards to help motivate yourself to stay focused. Make this year the best one it can be!

120 *Spend the Day at the Aquarium*

This is a great date for you and your loved one on a rainy day. Admission is usually a little steeper than desired; however, once inside, you'll realize it was worth the money. Taking a look at the incredible creatures that live all over the world in our deep ocean can help you appreciate your place on this earth. You'll feel like a kid as you watch the penguins swim, listen to the sea lions bark, or pick up a baby starfish. Don't be lazy; make sure to read the explanations and try to take five fun facts away from the experience. Did you know the oceans contain 99 percent of the living space on Earth?

121 *Go Out for Drinks or Dinner after Work*

We all need a moment of transition from the workday to home life. A quick drink or dinner with a coworker or friend will allow you to decompress from the stress of the day and calm you down for your relaxing evening. This also helps if you need to complain about that crazy coworker or the ridiculous assignment you were given and avoids bringing that energy back to your home. Your partner may wish you had come straight home, but will thank you in the end for not filling his ear with office drama.

122 *Clean Out Your Purse or Wallet*

Think of how much stuff you cram into your wallet or purse every day. Try to make this a quick, daily ritual when you arrive home from work. It will only take a few minutes to throw out the candy wrappers and receipts that you don't need. If you let this pile up, you will forget what gift card or important expense receipt you have left in there and may not find it until you are out of luck. You may want to create an envelope at home where you place all of your receipts to go through at a later time if it is too time-consuming for every day. This quick and easy daily chore will give you a sense of peace knowing that everything is in its place and you are organized.

123 *Savor Some Cotton Candy*

A must-have treat at any carnival or circus is delicious, fluffy cotton candy. You might not remember the appeal of the sticky treat, but the minute it melts in your mouth you will know why you had to have it. If you can't find a carnival or circus in your area, find a recipe online to make at home. Prepare to make a mess and have some fun! Make sure to celebrate National Cotton Candy Day on December 7.

124 Play Mini Golf

If you feel like being lazy but still want to do something rather than lie on the couch all day, try your swing at mini golf. This is nice way to get outside in the sunshine while enjoying some friendly competition with your friends. As an incentive, everyone should chip in to buy the winner's dinner that night. Don't forget your camera, as someone is bound to jump straight up in the air when they make that hole-in-one or fall into the small waterfall behind the putting green.

125 Write a Letter to a Deceased Family Member or Friend

There are so many things we wish we had said to or done with those that have passed on. Whether you feel you have unfinished business with a deceased loved one or simply want to speak with them, write a letter. It can be a quick note that states how much you miss and love them or a lengthy letter that tells them something you have always wanted to share. Sometimes the action of writing it all down can help you feel peace in your heart. They may not physically be able to read your words, but they will know what you wrote.

126 *Have a Nude Self-Portrait Taken*

We all must appreciate our bodies, no matter what size or shape; our bodies are our temples. Many choose to work out and diet their entire lives, but never take the moment to appreciate the work they have done. When choosing a photographer, make sure you have their complete trust, as these photos are for your personal use, not to be displayed on the Internet. You may choose to have a nice black-and-white print made to frame for your bedroom or have them all printed to create a photo album for those discretionary eyes to see. Whatever the purpose, these photos will continue to remind you how beautiful you are even with your imperfections. Take it off and show it off!

127 *Create a Relaxation Room*

Everyone needs a room in their house or apartment where they can just get away. This room isn't like your living room or bedroom; its specific purpose is for you to reflect or meditate, gather your thoughts, or just breathe. The most important aspect of the room is the ambiance. Use only candlelight, play some soft music, and burn incense if you like the smell of it. Paint the walls in a soft color like lavender or sea green. Use comfortable furniture like a papasan chair or even beanbags to sit in. Overstuffed pillows and soft blankets will make nice accents. Keep a journal or other creative materials there in case you feel inspired. If you live with another person or your family, you need your own personal space. Creating a relaxation room is the best way to have a space that's just for you.

128 Let Someone Brush Your Hair

You brush your hair every day, but it's a completely different experience when someone else does it for you. Ask a friend or partner to brush your hair. Have them use a large paddle brush so it makes your hair very soft. If they do it slowly and softly, it's enough to put you to sleep. Offer to return the favor; even if they have short hair, they are sure to enjoy this wonderful sensation.

129 Splurge on Snowplowing

If you live somewhere that experiences a snowy winter, you know it's not the first storm of the season that gets you down—it's the umpteenth time you're lacing up your boots to shovel that puts you over the edge. If you can't move to Hawaii, why not splurge on a plow service? You'll save yourself some back pain and cold toes, and have more time to enjoy hot chocolate and movies on the couch as you and your family watch the snow fall outside.

130 *Put Together a Puzzle*

Putting together a jigsaw puzzle can be really difficult depending on the pattern and number of pieces. Go out and buy one with a design you really like. This could be an all-day project, so it is best saved for a rainy day or if you are snowed in. When you are finished, you can glue all of the pieces together and put it in a frame. The great thing about puzzles is they come in a variety of challenge levels. You can do a 100-piece puzzle or a 1,000 piece, depending on how much time you have. If you really want a challenge, pick up a 3-D puzzle. You can have your very own model of the White House, Empire State Building, or the Millennium Falcon.

131 *Go Scuba Diving*

Exploring the incredible creatures of the deep is a one-of-a-kind experience. Snorkeling is always fun, but it doesn't allow you to take the time to truly appreciate what lies below. If you are not a certified diver, certification can take as few as three to four days. If you plan on taking scuba lessons on your vacation, try starting with the online courses to help eliminate time at the dive shop. Getting started is definitely an investment, as they recommend you purchase your own scuba gear for the lessons to help you feel more comfortable with gear fitted to you. Keep in mind that the minimum age requirement is ten years old, in case you are bringing your kids with you. Don't forget your sunscreen—you can get sunburned even underwater.

132 Don't Use Electricity on Earth Day

Earth Day is April 22, and what better way to show Earth some love than by turning off all electricity for the day. Commit to unplugging all electrical items in your house. There will, of course, be the exception of the refrigerator and other needed items, but try as hard as you can to keep it minimal. Try using mass transit or riding your bike to work that day to help cut down on your car pollution. Whatever you can do to cut back, do it on this day. This little bit of conservation will help the world, yourself, and many others to come. Check out your carbon footprint by visiting www.earthday.org.

133 Throw Yourself an Un-Birthday Party

If you've ever seen Disney's version of *Alice in Wonderland*, you will be familiar with un-birthday parties. The Mad Hatter and the March Hare are celebrating their un-birthdays when Alice finds them at their outrageous tea party. Your party doesn't need to be as ridiculous as theirs, but you can certainly follow their advice and have a wonderful party for yourself, even though it isn't your birthday. Tell your friends and family to come over and eat plenty of cake and ice cream. Presents are more than welcome. Everyone deserves more than one day all about them. Take advantage of your un-birthday!

134 Sleep on the Beach

Choose your favorite beach and the perfect summer night. You may decide to bring a sleeping bag or tent, but try to rough it as much as possible to enjoy the whole experience. Pack a small cooler of snacks and drinks so you are not tempted to leave. You may want to bring some binoculars to enjoy the stars. If it is approved with your local fire department, have a small campfire to roast marshmallows. Before falling asleep, put on some sunscreen just in case you sleep in. Curl up to your partner or best friend and fall asleep to the crashing waves and cool breeze on your face.

135 *Make Homemade Pizza*

When you make your own pizza at home, you can be as creative as you want. Go to the grocery store and pick up premade pizza dough, sauce, cheese, and all of your favorite toppings. Try to make one that you would never think to ask for at a pizza shop. This will become a weekly tradition at your house because it is so easy and cheaper than buying one. Making pizza is a great activity for kids, so if you have children get them involved. Or have some friends over and have a contest to see who can make the most delicious pizza.

136 *Back Up Your Work*

This quick and easy task can help you avoid the inevitable crash and painful realization that your whole life of work and fun is gone! Although always recommended, so many people still do not back up their work and lose it all, especially today with people saving their entire music library and photo albums on the computer. Spend the money, purchase an external hard drive, and back up your media and documents. Remember, even though it might be a grueling process, it will benefit you in the long run and give you that rest-assured feeling that your lifetime of computer work is safe.

137 *Have Breakfast in Bed*

If you don't have someone that can make you breakfast in bed, you can still enjoy it by yourself. Plan what you want to have the night before and get as much prepared as you can. You can mix pancake batter the night before and leave it in the fridge. Or put a bagel in the toaster so you just have to press the button when you wake up. If you have a timer on your coffee pot, you could wake up to the smell of fresh coffee. As soon as breakfast is done, jump right back into bed and enjoy your meal. You could even fall back to sleep when you are done or read the morning paper.

138 *Learn How to Play a Musical Instrument*

It is never too late to learn how to play an instrument. Choose something that will work for you in your daily life. If you can't afford to buy a piano but want to learn how to play, there are plenty of inexpensive keyboards you can purchase. If you are someone that would like to take your instrument with you, try learning how to play the guitar or violin. It doesn't matter what instrument you choose; any of them will help expand your mind and help you focus your energy on something other than your stress. If you can't afford to take proper lessons, you can find many tutorials online where you can teach yourself.

139 *Have Sex in the Woods*

There are plenty of places outside to get down and dirty, but having sex in the woods offers a few features that make it a special experience. If you are deep in the woods, the chances of being interrupted or caught are slim. You can hide behind a large tree or in between big rocks. You can have a bit of privacy even though you are outside. You might find that the smell of the trees and clean air is somewhat of an aphrodisiac. Doing a natural act in nature is exhilarating. Grab your partner and head to the woods today. Bring a blanket so you can be comfortable on the ground. Beware of poisonous plants—you don't want to have to explain to your doctor how you got poison ivy on your naughty bits.

140 *Hire a Landscaper*

If you don't have a knack for cutting grass in a straight line or trimming shrubs, hire a landscaper. Find a reputable company by reviewing testimonials online for local companies or ask around the neighborhood. They will give your lawn and shrubbery a perfect manicure. If you don't know what plants or flowers would look best in your yard, get a consultation from a gardener as well. A nice landscape can add value to your home as it raises curbside appeal.

141 Buy a New Toothbrush

The American Dental Association recommends you buy a new toothbrush every three to four months. If you are way past that mark, go out and buy a new one today. Find one you really like. If you've been wanting to try an electric toothbrush, get one. Brushing your teeth is one of the most important things you have to do each day, but it won't do any good with a worn-down toothbrush. While you are out, buy some new floss and mouthwash. You can't be too careful—they're the only set of teeth you have.

142 Share a Taxi with a Stranger

If you see someone else hailing a cab, ask them where they are going. Half of the time they will be going in at least the same direction. By sharing the cab, you will cut down on cost and added pollution from another car. Putting that positive energy out there will help boost your spirit and that of others around you. This energy will domino throughout both of your days and inspire many others to reach out and help a fellow human.

143 Carve Pumpkins

You are never too old to enjoy some Halloween fun! Carving pumpkins into jack o' lanterns is the ultimate Halloween activity. You may want to invite a few friends over to enjoy some wine and Halloween-themed appetizers for your carving experience. To help keep the pumpkin fresh and looking frightful, spread some petroleum jelly or cooking oil over the design. Have some toothpicks handy to help reattach any of those pieces you accidentally cut off. Try to be as creative as possible. You can even hold a contest in your neighborhood.

144 Visit a Different Country

Make it a goal to visit a different country this year. Whether it is a neighboring country close to home or overseas, seeing the way other cultures live their lives is truly an eye-opening experience. Remember that a vacation is not always relaxing, and you should map out times for rest and for exploring. When preparing for your trip, do research on the country's currency, language, and customs. Try to familiarize yourself with their laws and regulations to stay out of trouble. Always know where your nearest U.S. embassy is located in case of an emergency. Finally, make sure you have a large and empty memory card for all those memorable snapshots.

145 *Kiss Someone on New Year's Eve*

New Year's Eve can be one of the best or one of the worst holidays; it all depends on whether you have someone to kiss at the end of the night to ring in the New Year. At the end of the night people start pairing off, counting down the final seconds of the year, holding someone close. If you don't have a boyfriend or girlfriend tonight, kiss a friend or a perfect stranger. Who cares who you slide lips with tonight . . . drink some bubbly and pucker up!

146 *Start a Neighborhood Baseball Team*

Who can resist America's favorite pastime? Break out the bats and gloves and start a baseball team in your neighborhood. This is a great way to meet your neighbors if you don't already know them, and get some exercise. Post fliers or go door to door to see if anyone is interested. If it's successful, think about starting a town league with other neighborhoods joining in. It could be a great time.

147 Watch the Tides Change

One of the most amazing things that happen on Earth every day is the changing of the tides. The tides are controlled by the gravitational pull of the moon; they go in and out a number of times during the day. Head down to the beach today to watch the tides change. You can check the newspaper or go online to read the tide charts, those handy daily updates that let you know when the tides go in and out. Bring a chair so you can sit right at the water's edge. The tides change slowly, so enjoy your time with your feet in the water.

148 Make Homemade Doughnuts

Fresh, homemade doughnuts are better than anything you'll find at your local coffee shop, and are relatively easy to make. Decide if you want to make cake-like doughnuts or light, airy ones. There are a number of recipes for dough, so find a delicious one online or in your favorite cookbook. The only equipment you need is a deep fryer. If you don't have a stand-alone fryer, just use a large, deep pan. Start by filling the pan with vegetable oil. Make sure the oil is very hot before you drop the dough in—it should be about 370°F. Make sure they are golden brown on one side before you flip them. When they are fully cooked, shake them in a brown bag with granulated sugar and cinnamon. The smell of these delicious treats will wake everyone. Make them this morning and enjoy with a hot cup of tea or coffee.

149 Turn Off the Television

Americans watch over five hours of television a day. Do yourself a favor and turn off the tube for twenty-four hours. You might think you would be bored to tears, but make a list of all the things you can do when you're not wasting time watching television. Do a little home decorating or try a new recipe. Start a new novel or write one of your own. Invite some friends over for a night of fun. Nothing on television is better than spending time with loved ones.

150 Use the Snooze Button

Ever have one of those mornings where you just don't want to wake up? Well, if today is one of those days, hit the snooze button on your alarm clock. Sure, it's only another ten or fifteen minutes, but it's well worth it. Don't worry about running a little behind schedule; if you don't do it all the time, it shouldn't be that big of a deal. Indulge in a few more minutes of shuteye and you'll feel better about getting things done later in the day.

. . . .

151 Write a Thank-You Letter to Your Parent(s)

Take a moment today to write a quick note of thanks to your parents. It could be a letter explaining your love and gratitude for all their support over the years or a simple thank you for the dinner they put on the table. It doesn't matter what age you are, it is important to thank them for their unconditional love. Try not to send this note on their birthday, anniversary, or holiday, but on a random day where it will take them by surprise. This note will fill their hearts and will remind them of what a good job they did raising you. Include a recent photo of yourself to personalize it.

. . . .

152 Give a Hands-Free Massage to Your Lover

Here's a new twist for your foreplay lineup: A massage doesn't have to be given with the hands. Use every part of your body to rub him down. Using your feet, chest, thighs, and elbows, squeeze the tension out of each other. There are a few types of oil that you can use to make things more fun. You can buy some warming or flavored massage oil or just plain old baby oil. Before you both strip down, cover the bed with a few old sheets that you don't mind getting greasy. To add to the mood, light a few of your favorite scented candles. Take your time and be creative.

....

153 *Buy One New Piece of Furniture*

Purchasing a piece of furniture for your home is always a good investment, as it brings character and value to your house. Sometimes, the pure pleasure of buying something new for your home will lift your spirits. Whether it is an inexpensive decoration or a luxurious bed or couch, take the time to do your research. An impulse buy is always fun, but making sure it fits into the overall picture of that specific room is key. When purchasing large items, make sure you are ready for the delivery by measuring the dimensions of your doorways to confirm it will fit. A last-minute unhinging of a door could take away from the fun!

154 *Change Your Hair Color*

It is time to switch things up and try a new hair color. Your hair will always grow and can always be cut, so try something different this time. It is helpful for you and the hair stylist to bring a few pictures of what you are looking for. You may consider going darker in the fall and winter and lightening things up for the spring and summer. Avoid making changes before a big event such as a family reunion or wedding. If the transition doesn't go as planned, you want that needed time to make the right adjustments. If dyeing your hair is out of the question, try purchasing some hair extensions to mix in some color and desired length. There are reasonably priced clip-in hair extensions, but make sure to go for the real hair for a better look. Take a look at www.hairuwear.com for some suggestions.

155 *Start a Block Party*

Knock on your neighbors' doors or send around an e-mail and organize a neighborhood block party! What better way to meet some new friends and enjoy the spring or summer than a potluck, BYOB, dancing-in-the-street-bash? Who knows—you may even start a tradition!

156 Watch Disney Movies

You can always count on a Disney movie to make your heart smile and maybe even bring a tear to your eye. Choose one of the classics like *Cinderella*, *Sleeping Beauty*, *Pinocchio*, or *Snow White*, all which were released before 1959. Cuddle up on the couch with your favorite childhood snack and lose yourself in the fantasy. You will be surprised at how many of the songs you can sing along with!

157 Drive Across the Country

Road trips are always a fun and exciting way to get somewhere. You can plan on taking a long road trip or driving a rental car or Winnebago to a desired location and flying back home. When renting a Winnebago or camper, you can avoid the hotel prices and enjoy more of the great outdoors that this country has to offer. You may want to invite a few friends and create a video diary of your entire trip for everyone to have when finished. Before you leave, draw out a route with planned overnight stops and places of interest. Whether it's from New York to L.A. or Miami to Seattle, driving across this beautiful country will be a rewarding trip with plenty of memorable moments. Make sure you know how to change a tire!

158 *Play an April Fool's Joke*

You are never too old for this one! If you are in a work environment, make sure to choose a joke that will not interfere too much with the professional work at hand. Depending on your office culture, you will be able to gauge just how far you can go. Go dressed to work with all of your clothes inside out. Many will think you have made a mistake and be embarrassed to say anything. Just watching them squirm will give you the last laugh. Whatever you do, plan ahead; a joke gone wrong can sometimes lead to disaster.

159 *Let Someone Set You Up on a Date*

If dating websites are not working and you are sick of going to the same bar or club on Friday night, let someone else do the work. You will be surprised by what your friends and loved ones can do when put to the matchmaking test. Try not to give them any ideas of what you are looking for in a person; let them take the lead and see what they come up with. Remember, your friends are part of different circles and may see a potential match that you are not even aware of. Allow them to set up the location of the date to take you out of your comfort zone. Even if the date is awful, you haven't lost anything and have done hardly any work getting there.

160   *Ride a Horse in the Woods*

Horses have been known to have a very special connection to humans. For hundreds of years, we've relied on horses for transportation and even friendship. Like many animals, they have a keen instinct that lets them know how we are feeling. Today, find a horse farm that offers horseback riding on a trail through the woods. When you are riding a particularly sensitive horse, you will feel like you are being protected. Your horse will make sure you are safe while you are enjoying the ride. If you show them respect, they will do the same. Being in nature with an animal can be a very spiritual experience. Take in how nice it feels to be riding outside in the fresh air. Be sure to stroke and pet the horse so the horse feels comfortable. Ask the lead rider if you can give the horse a treat when you get back, like some carrots or sugar cubes, to show your appreciation.

161   *Have Frozen Hot Chocolate in the Summer*

If you need a hot chocolate fix but it's the middle of summer, make it frozen! You'll need the following ingredients:

4 ounces your favorite chocolate
2 teaspoons hot chocolate mix
1½ tablespoons sugar
1½ cups milk
3 cups ice

Cut your chocolate into pieces. Melt it in a saucepan, stirring. Add the hot chocolate mix and sugar and continue stirring until completely blended. Turn off the heat and add ½ cup milk and continue stirring. Once cooled to room temperature, pour the mixture into a blender with the rest of the milk and ice. Blend on high until it has the consistency of a frozen drink. Enjoy your frozen hot chocolate while sitting out in the hot summer sun!

162 *Buy New Workout Clothes*

It can be difficult to find the motivation to exercise. Buying new clothes to work out in often does the trick. Pick out something you feel comfortable in and something that will show off all of the hard work you are doing. If you need new sneakers, pick those up as well. It is very important to have sneakers that give you the correct support so you don't injure yourself. New clothes will give you a boost of confidence as well.

163 Heat Your Sheets Before You Go to Bed

Kramer from *Seinfeld* once used a pizza oven to warm his clothes before putting them on. This indulgence is a little less crazy, but just as comforting. Before going to bed, put your sheets and blankets in the dryer. When they are warm enough, quickly make your bed and jump in. You'll feel like you are in a warm cocoon and be out like a light in no time. Another version of this is throwing one soft blanket in the dryer before you sit down to watch a movie or read a book. It's sure to keep you warm in the winter or any time you are chilly.

164 Write Your Memoir

We all have a story to tell, and one of the most cathartic things to do is get it out. Make an outline that highlights the major events of your life. Think of the most important thing that has happened to you and focus your story on that. Everyone is unique and everyone is interesting in their own way. Find out what has made your life different and what has made you who you are. This memoir can be just for you; you don't have to show it to anyone else if you don't want to. If you are very ambitious, try writing your family's history. Reflecting on your past will make you appreciate what's to come.

165 *Go Commando All Day*

Sometimes those undies can feel too confining. Break free today and go commando! To avoid the inevitable sweating and chafing on a steamy, summer day, a light dusting of baby powder will do the trick. This naughty little secret will make you feel sexy today. Ladies, when spring arrives and you break out the skirts, let your body breathe. By going au *naturale* today, you'll be turned on and avoid panty lines at the same time. Enjoy a wedgie-free day!

166 *Clean Out and Organize Your Closet*

Do you have shoes from ten years ago or sweaters that you have never worn sitting in your closet? If so, it is time for a little spring cleaning! First, clean out all of the clothes and shoes that you no longer wear or want. Make sure to donate them to charity as opposed to throwing them away. Next, purchase a bunch of matching hangers to give your closet a clean and organized look. Organize your clothes by the seasons so you can easily find that warm sweater or light polo shirt. When you are done, you will not only feel less cluttered but you will save that precious time before work when you could be snoozing.

167 Take a Bath Filled with Flowers

Go to your local florist and pick out the sweetest-smelling flowers you can find. Whether it is some simple rose petals or lilac blossoms, your bathtub will look and smell like a spring garden. Before jumping in, cut off all stems and prickly thorns. To add even more fragrance, find a bath oil that complements the flowers you have chosen. After the tub is filled, place the flowers on the water's surface to create a luxurious blanket of petals. As you ease into the water, let the aroma and warmth overwhelm your senses and ease your mind.

168 Send a Drink to an Attractive Stranger

While it may seem intimidating, the next time you spot a handsome guy or pretty girl at a bar or restaurant, have the bartender send over a cocktail or glass of wine—your treat. The worst that can happen is you lose some money. The best? Well, who knows where the night may lead?

169 *Have a Board Game Party*

Monopoly. Clue. Scrabble. These beloved board games are reason enough to throw a party. Tonight, invite a group of friends over and have them each bring their favorite game. Encourage them to think beyond the classics so you have a wide variety. Everyone should bring something as a prize for the winner of each game. Feel free to create your own rules or add a new twist to an old game, like strip checkers or drunken chess.

170 *Go Snorkeling*

If you are a little hesitant to try scuba diving but still want to swim with the fishies, go snorkeling. Before heading out, lather up with a high-SPF suntan lotion. Don't forget that your backside will be exposed to the sun, but you won't feel the intense heat while you are in the water. When you go snorkeling, you will be given a pair of flippers, snorkel, and mask. Make sure everything fits properly before you jump in. If you are an inexperienced swimmer and nervous, stay close to the instructor and boat, as the currents can be unsuspectingly strong. Getting up close and personal with the incredible sea life below is an experience not to be missed.

171   *Send Out Valentines*

Valentine's Day isn't just for lovers, it's for everyone you care about. Send a Valentine to your parents, siblings, grandparents, and friends. Let them know you love and appreciate them not just on February 14, but every day of the year. If you want to send something special, make heart-shaped cookies and decorate them with red sprinkles or red frosting. Remember how blessed you are to have so many people in your life that love you, too.

172   *Have a Tree-Trimming Party*

Getting a tree at Christmas is a classic tradition. Invite your friends and family over to trim the tree and have everyone bring an ornament to add to your tree. Serve eggnog and gingerbread cookies, play Christmas music, or watch holiday movies. Have your guests cover the tree with lights, tinsel, and don't forget the star or angel on top. This is a great way to ring in the season.

173 *Go Fishing*

Fishing can be one of the most relaxing and exhilarating activities in nature. It is not always about the catch, but the minutes and hours leading up to that moment, that can be the most rewarding. Today, grab your fishing pole and head out to the nearest lake or river. Nature provides you with that needed silence. It is a time for a parent and child to bond or two friends to reminisce. Whether sitting on a calm lake in a canoe or standing in the surf of the crashing waves, you will experience the beauty of the water around you and enjoy the company of loved ones.

174 *Eat Juicy, Ripe Fruit in the Shower*

There are a few varieties of fruit that can get really messy if you eat them when they are ripe. The juice from pineapples, oranges, watermelon, and peaches can run down your chin, neck, and arms and make you very sticky. To truly enjoy these luscious fruits, eat them in the shower. Strip down and take one of your favorite messy fruits with you. Don't worry about becoming covered in juice and pulp; it will all wash off as you eat. If you happen to be on vacation at a beach, try the same thing in the ocean. Being able to let loose and be a slob for a little while is what counts here.

175 *Start a Piggy Bank*

You know all of that loose change on the floor of your car or in between the cushions of your couch? It can add up! Start a piggy bank to collect all of that change. Collect it for a year and watch your savings grow. You just might be able to take that vacation you've been thinking about. Add to it whenever you can; if you have a few extra singles in your pocket, throw those in as well. At the end of the year, you'll have a nice chunk of change to do with what you will.

176 *Make a Lottery Wish List*

You might not win the lottery in your lifetime, but you can still dream about what you would do with the winnings. Pretend you've won a million dollars. Then write down how you would use the money, what trips you would take, what bills you would pay off, and who you would share it with. A million dollars might not seem like a lot of money by today's standards, but to you it could make a world of difference. You could go back and finish school or take that dream trip to Europe with your family. You could buy a new car or even a summer home. Or if you invest it wisely, you'll never have to work again. Even if you never win, you can wish.

177 Change One Thing You Don't Like about Yourself

We all have one thing we don't like about ourselves. Maybe you worry too much or are afraid to take a risk. Maybe you want to eat healthier or want to commit to incorporating exercise into your daily routine. Today, make the commitment to change—there's no better time than the present. If you are thinking, "It's too late, I'm too old to change," think again; it's never too late to improve yourself. It won't be easy at first, so take it one step at a time. Just saying "Yes, I'm ready to change that part of my life" is a huge step.

178 Make Out at the Movies

Feeling like a couple of horny teenagers? Take it to the movies. Plan to see a late-morning or early-afternoon show so the chances of getting an empty theater are greater. Forget the popcorn and soda this time—butter hands and burping are not hot. Instead, pick up some chocolate-covered mints at the concession stand, which will leave a sweet and fresh taste in your mouth. Head to the last row so you can easily hide in the shadows with your honey. When the lights dim, get down to business; try to see how far you can go without being caught. It's a little dangerous, but a lot of fun.

179 Take Inspiration from Home Magazines to Decorate

If you are looking for some interesting ways to decorate your house, look no further than your favorite home magazines. Pick up a three-ring binder and some plastic protective sleeves and create an idea book filled with pages from the magazines. You should organize your idea book by the rooms in your home so when it comes time to renovate that particular room, you will have a slate of fresh ideas. These pictures can be shown to your decorator and contractor to help guide them in the right direction.

180 Splurge on a Pedicure

Having someone soak, scrub, and polish your feet is a true indulgence. Make an appointment today for a pedicure. If you've never had one before, you are in for a real treat. You will be treated to a warm soak in a bubbling footbath. Take this time to relax and let the stress melt from your body, Once your feet are sufficiently soft, your pedicurist will scrub the dead skin off the soles of your feet and trim your toe nails. You will then get a foot massage with peppermint lotion. If you are getting your nails painted, you'll choose a color. One thing to remember is to bring a pair of sandals or flip-flops to wear if you are planning on getting your nails painted—you don't want to smudge the wet paint by putting on shoes. Pedicures can get pricey, but they are well worth it.

181 *Make an Herb Box*

Fresh herbs are a healthy way to brighten up any meal, so why not grow your own? You can pick up a flower box at your local hardware store or if you are familiar with woodworking, make one yourself. You can paint it or decorate it to match the colors of your house if you're feeling extra creative. Fill the box with potting soil and choose herbs you enjoy. Plant some parsley, sage, rosemary, and thyme, or perhaps some oregano and basil. Herb plants are inexpensive, and you'll taste the fruits of your labor for months to come.

182 *Play Your Favorite Childhood Video Game*

If you grew up between the '70s and '90s, you probably have fond memories of Pong, Pac-Man, Super Mario Bros., and Tetris. Like many of that generation's youth, you spent countless hours on Atari and Nintendo. Today, relive your childhood and play some of the classics. You can go out and buy an old console and some cartridges or play them online. Many video game stores sell refurbished game consoles or you can easily find them on eBay. Visit *www.everyvideogame.com* to find Nintendo games online for free!

183 *Take a Hot-Air Balloon Ride*

Soar high in the sky today in a hot-air balloon ride. If it is a nice day and you don't have a fear of heights, you're in for an exhilarating experience. A hot-air balloon works by using heated air to lift it off the ground and fly higher and higher. The hot air makes the balloon buoyant because it has a lower density than the cold air outside the balloon. A propane burner is used to heat the air. You sit in a basket made of wicker or rattan that is attached to the balloon. When the operator turns off the flame, the balloon will go down. If you are a little nervous, ask your operator to explain what he is doing throughout the trip. You'll feel more secure if you know how it works.

184 *Color Easter Eggs*

To celebrate the season of spring or the Easter holiday, color some eggs. This is a very old tradition that is still practiced to welcome springtime. You can buy a coloring kit at your local grocery store. The kit will provide different shades of egg dye in the form of tablets. Follow the instructions and dissolve the tablets in water and vinegar. The pungent vinegar smell is sure to bring back childhood memories of this activity. When the eggs are colored, you can decorate them with stickers or draw on them with markers. Let your artistic abilities shine and make some beautiful eggs. You can eat them for breakfast later.

185 Set Single Friends Up on a Date

If you have two friends you think would be perfect for each other, set them up on a date. To take the pressure off, throw a party at your place and invite both of them. Before they come over, think of things they have in common. When you introduce them, you can bring it up so they can easily start a conversation. Being a matchmaker can be fun, but if something goes wrong you could end up in the middle of things. Try to be diplomatic—don't take sides. If things go right, you'll feel good knowing you brought love into their lives.

186 Find Shapes in the Clouds

If you are in need of some relaxation and want to enjoy the nice weather, lie down in the grass and take a look at the clouds.

With a friend, create a game of who can point out the most shapes and objects. You may want to reward more points for specific cartoon characters or animals as opposed to shapes and letters. Lying there and watching the clouds roll by can even whisk you away into a quick nap. This may seem juvenile, but allowing your brain to rest from the daily stress and focus your energy somewhere else can recharge your mind and give you motivation to get through the rest of the day.

187 *Drink Good Coffee*

Life's too short to drink bad coffee. If you're used to drinking the cheap stuff, splurge today and buy some premium coffee. One of the most expensive and sought-after coffees available is Kona coffee from Hawaii. You can order some online at *www.konacoffee.com*. If you need a coffee fix right now, hit up some of the local coffee shops and sample their brews. Find your favorite so you know where to go in your neighborhood. Grocery stores carry many brands and flavors; buy a few varieties and make some at home. Coffee is a simple luxury that can be enjoyed every day. Don't settle for less than the best.

188 Get a Library Card

If you love books, movies, or music, you should be going to your library on a weekly basis. Books, movies, and music for free! If you don't already have a library card, get one today. Try to figure out how much money you would save at the end of the year by taking advantage of your local public library. Many libraries now let you order from other libraries in the area so you have a larger variety of things to choose from, and they will deliver what you want to your local branch. Libraries don't get a lot of money from the government, so donate whenever you can or think about holding a fundraiser in your town to show your appreciation.

189 Fantasize about Your Wedding

We all dream about our wedding day: the flowers, the food, the music, our new spouse. If you've never been married and have never thought about what you really want on your special day, write it all down. No one has to see it; this is just for you. Find pictures online of your favorite wedding dresses, create the perfect menu for you and your guests, make a playlist of the songs you want to dance to. Pretend that money is no object and you can have anything and everything you want. If you want a famous singer or celebrity to show up . . . it's done. This isn't about practicality; it's about fun.

190 Keep a Book of Funny Quotes from Family and Friends

If you are not into taking the time to write a daily journal but want to commemorate something funny your loved one said or did, try keeping a book of quotes. If you write them down with a quick description of the person and setting, you will be able to go back years later and reminisce about that exact moment in time. You may want to keep a physical book or running document on the computer. If you are out, text or e-mail yourself the quote so you can include it when you get home. After many years, you could have the pages bound and given as a gift to your family or close friends to remember the funny times.

191 *Buy a Waterproof Vibrator*

Want to have some fun in the bathtub or shower? Buy a waterproof vibrator from an adult novelty shop or online. They come in all shapes, sizes, and colors . . . and even glow in the dark! There are ones that fit in the palm of your hand—perfect for using in the pool or the ocean if you are on vacation. No one will ever know what you're up to. Stick to vibrators that you will use externally; you will avoid needing a silicon-based lubricant, which would take away from being discreet.

192 *Get a Pool*

Whether you decide on a kiddie pool or an in-ground, you will be supplied with some cool water and many memories during the hot months. The price of a pool can be as low as $50 to as high as you want to spend. The options today are truly limitless, and you can create almost anything you dream of. Whether it is a tropical paradise or the traditional rectangular above-ground pool, do not be fooled by the luxury of it all. Pools are a lot of work and the upkeep is expensive with the winterization process and keeping it clean during the summer months. Before deciding on a pool, make sure you are ready for the expenses and the work that goes along with it.

193 Get a Free Makeover at a Cosmetics Counter

Chances are if you've ever been in a department store, you've been hounded by the women at the cosmetic counter to try a new shade of lipstick or blush. This time, instead of walking right on by, sit down for a free makeover. Pretend you don't know anything about makeup or what looks good on you. They will be more than willing to help and try different products. You'll probably learn some helpful tips and tricks if you don't know them already, like the perfect shade of base or the best way to blend eye shadows. It's fun to have someone do your makeup for you, so give it a try. Of course, they'll push you to buy something, but if you really can't afford it just say you'll come back another time.

194 Hang Up a Flattering Picture of Yourself

Most of us hate the way we look in photos. So it's always a nice surprise when we're pleased by the way we look in a picture! Why not quiet that voice telling you not to be vain and print out the picture? Whether you hang it on your fridge or keep it in your desk drawer at work, you have an easy way to boost yourself when you're feeling down. Simply take a quick glimpse and remind yourself that the good-looking person in the photo is you. Watch out, world!

195 *Play Catch*

Playing catch is such a simple game: tossing a ball back and forth in the backyard or on the beach. Yet it can be relaxing as well as fun. Today, find your old baseball mitts or borrow them from a friend and play a game of catch. On a warm spring day, this is a perfect outdoor activity. You won't work up a sweat, but you're still getting exercise. You can even play with your dog if you have one. Or you can round up the kids in your neighborhood and have one big game.

196 *Get Tickets to a Playoff Game*

Show your team pride and get tickets to a playoff game. This might seem near impossible, but if you know where to look you'll be able to find them. Check *www.craigslist.org* to see if anyone is selling tickets at the last minute. Ask friends or coworkers if they know anyone selling tickets. As a last resort, show up at the game and see if anyone is selling tickets outside; this might turn into a little adventure. Try to surprise a loved one if they are a fan as well. Wear your team jersey and get ready to cheer!

197 *Create Your Own Holiday*

Just as Frank Costanza created Festivus on *Seinfeld* and Seth Cohen of *The O.C.* created Chrismukkah, you, too, can create your own holiday. Try to think of an event or person you would like to celebrate and research whether there is a day devoted to it. September 19 is Talk Like a Pirate Day and February 24 is International Pancake Day. With strange holidays like these, you have full permission to make one of your own. Have your family observe it for years to come. If it's truly important to you, take the day off work to celebrate.

198 *Play Poker with Friends*

A little Texas Hold 'Em can turn a dull Tuesday night into a party. Invite some friends over to play poker tonight. Chips and dip, nachos, mini sandwiches, and plenty of beer are perfect poker fare. You might walk away with a pocketful of your friend's cash. Try not to win every round though . . . you want them to come back for another game.

199 Lie Down in the Light of the Full Moon

For centuries, it has been believed that the full moon has a strange effect on human behavior. It has been blamed for violence, temporary insanity, insomnia, feelings of lust, and magical phenomena associated with werewolves. Some neopagans celebrate the full moon by holding rituals called esbats every month. It is seen as a very powerful time of the month. Tonight, lie down outside on your porch or in your yard—wherever you can see the full moon clearly—in the light of the full moon. If you have a telescope, look at the moon up close. Try to see if you feel any different by watching the full moon. If you start to howl . . . go back inside.

200 Make S'mores in Your Backyard

These delightful treats are a must-have at any campout; however, you can still enjoy them even if you're at home in your backyard. Go to the store and buy graham crackers, chocolate bars, and marshmallows. The big marshmallows are easier to work with when it comes to s'mores. If you plan on making a fire pit in your yard, you'll need some firewood as well. Roast the marshmallows on sticks or if you are in a pinch, an unraveled coat hanger will work as well. Stick a few squares of chocolate on the graham and the mallow on top of the chocolate. It's best to wait until the chocolate has melted a bit before you take a bite. Have some friends over to share the treats or eat them all yourself. Either way, it's gooey, chocolatey fun.

201 Take a Class for Fun at a Local College

If you've always wanted to take a creative writing course or a class on Western civilization, sign up today at your local college. If you haven't been to school in a long time, don't be nervous; you'll find many students just like you are either going for a degree or just want to learn something new. Since this is just for fun, it takes the pressure off when it comes to tests and finals. You'll want to do well, but at least you don't need this class to graduate. Learning shouldn't stop just because you are no longer in school. Get a list of the courses offered and pick one that sounds interesting.

202 Take a Mental Health Day

With all of the stress that follows us day to day, sometimes you just need to recuperate and rebalance yourself. A mental health day does just that. Take the day off from work today and decompress: go shopping, eat out for lunch, do yoga, get a massage. Erase responsibility and stress from your life for twenty-four hours. You'll come back to work feeling refreshed and ready to take on anything.

203 Count Your Blessings

Get out a piece of paper today and try to count your blessings. You may need a whole notebook, but write down everything that you are grateful for. Depending on how many you write, type them up, print them out, and cut each one out. Place them all in a bowl and grab one every day just before you leave the house. On your way to work or on your lunch break, take a moment to reflect on that item. If you can, use that blessing to help inspire and motivate you to do something nice for someone else today.

204 Have Sex on Your Lunch Break

Use that half hour to your advantage, and have a quickie on your lunch break. Most of the time will be taken up finding the right place, so try to plan that ahead of time so you can focus on the task at hand. Have your partner meet you at your secret place. Make sure you have lubricant, condoms, or any other accessories ready to go. You'll go back to work with a boost of energy and a glowing face. If anyone asks, just say you went for a facial.

205 Declutter Your Attic and Basement

You will be surprised to see how much stuff you have collected in your attic and basement over the years. Many of these things you will never need, but for some reason you have that just-in-case mentality. By decluttering these spaces, you will feel the energy in your home get better. You may even find those ice skates you have been searching for or the old photo album that you thought you lost. Take today to clean out your storage places and try to cut your precious junk in half. Remember that donating to charity is very important, as one person's junk is another's treasure.

206 Buy Cashmere

Cashmere is a wool fiber from the Cashmere goat. Soft cashmere against your skin feels heavenly, but it can also cost a fortune. If you can't afford a cashmere sweater, buy a pair of gloves or a scarf. If you shop at discount stores, you might be able to find cashmere at a considerably lower price. Wearing an article of cashmere will make you feel luxurious inside and out. Splurge on some today.

207 *Flirt with a Firefighter*

Is there anything hotter than a firefighter in uniform? Treat yourself and your local heroes by stopping by the firehouse with a dish for them to eat—and enjoy the flirtation that comes your way. Firefighters love to eat, but with their unpredictable schedule finding time to cook while at work is hard. Tonight, make enough food for all of the firefighters on duty and bring it to your local fire station. They will love a hearty, home-cooked meal—and you'll love their grateful attention.

208 *Finger Paint*

The reason finger painting is so much fun now that you're an adult is the same reason it was when you were in preschool: You're allowed to make a big, sloppy mess. Get a large piece of heavy-stock paper or paperboard and a few different bottles of paint. Pour the paint on the paper and let your fingers glide through the wet paint with no rhyme or reason. Blend colors together to make new colors, create designs, or just enjoy the feel of the paint on your hands.

209 *Swim with Dolphins*

If you live in or are visiting Florida anytime soon, one activity you have to do is swim with the dolphins. There are many dolphin education facilities that allow you to get in the water with these incredible creatures. Do some research to find out where you can swim with them. This is truly an amazing and unique experience. Dolphins are very smart animals and have been trained to follow specific commands to give you a real show. They have been known to be protective of humans, so you can feel safe in their habitat. When you get into the water, you'll be able to touch them and they might even give you a kiss. You can grab onto their dorsal fin and they will pull you along for a nice ride.

210 *Dress Up for Halloween*

Wearing costumes and masks at Halloween is an ancient custom people performed because they believed the veil between the spirit world and our world was thin on Halloween night. If they wore costumes or masks, they could trick ghosts and evil spirits into thinking they were one of them and they would remain unharmed. Now, wearing costumes is all in good fun. Think of a unique costume and wear it on Halloween. If your office allows it, wear it to work and have a costume competition. Or wear it to answer the door when children come to trick-or-treat.

211 *Have a Candle Party*

One of the best-known direct sellers of candles that offer candle parties is Partylite. Visit *www.partylite.com* to find a consultant in your area so you can learn how to host a candle party. Invite as many friends as you can over to see the demonstration and purchase candles and accessories. When you host a party, you will receive a percentage of the party's total to use toward your own purchases. Depending on how many people order candles, you get them for free! There are also plenty of hostess specials where you can get candles and accessories for half the price or less. This is a great way to throw a little party and walk away with a lot of free stuff.

212 *Build Your Own Bird Feeder*

One of the best things about the beginning of spring is hearing and seeing the birds of the season. Winter is over and they're out and about looking for food for their new chicks. Help them out and build a bird feeder. Find a picture of one you like online and try to imitate it. Be sure to leave a hole in the front so they can fly in and get their birdseed. If you aren't skilled with nails and wood, buy one that is unfinished and paint and decorate it yourself. Buy some birdseed and place it outside your kitchen window. You'll be able to see your new friends every day.

213 *Sample All of the Flavors at Your Local Ice Cream Shop*

Do you ever worry about ordering a flavor you've never had before and not liking it? Why waste the money when you can sample the flavor before you buy. This is an easy way to save money and get your ice cream fill. They usually keep small sampling spoons nearby, so ask to try all of the flavors. If you are worried about seeming suspicious, tell them you are writing an article on the best ice cream flavor and it will help with your research. You'll be able to walk out of there without paying a dime. Be sure to leave a tip for their trouble.

214 Put Photos in Albums

Do you have piles and stacks of photos in the corner of your room? Get them in an album as soon as possible. Not only does this organize them, it helps protect them from folding or getting ruined. If you have your entire photo album neatly organized on your computer, make time to have it printed. The computer is a great place to store these memories, but having them in a hard, tangible form makes it easier to share with others and gives you the assurance of a backup.

215 Give Yourself a Foot Massage Using Reflexology

A foot massage can feel like heaven, but did you know that it can benefit other parts of the body as well? Reflexology is the practice of massaging specific areas of the feet in order to affect other parts of your body. Along with acupuncture and Reiki, reflexology works by changing the flow of a person's chi, or life-force energy, to promote healing. Different areas of the foot correspond with different body systems. For example, the tops of your toes correspond with your brain; the inner arch of the foot matches the stomach; and the lower foot and heel match with the colon and bladder. Look online for a map of the foot and the body parts affected when you massage them.

You can give yourself a massage. If you have a stomachache and massage the right area of the foot, you will feel better after the rub.

216 Make a Playlist of Relaxation Music

If you can't seem to relax and need extra help, create a mix of music that will transition you into that peaceful mood. Choose songs that help you calm down. Be mindful not to include those slow melodies that remind you of sad memories. Organize the songs from the fastest tempo to the slowest, and consider starting with lyric songs and ending with some classical. This natural progression will assist you in slowing down. Make yourself a cup of tea or pour a nice glass of wine, sit back, and enjoy the serene melodies.

217 Take a Belly Dancing Class

Belly dancing is an ancient Middle Eastern dance form. The origins and reasons behind belly dancing aren't fully known and are debated among scholars. Some believe it was done by both men and women as a social dance; others believe women only practiced it as a way to celebrate their sensuality and the power of being a woman. No one will argue that belly dancing is not sensual in nature. The music, costumes, and movements are all hypnotic—you can't help but feel under a spell when you watch or practice belly dancing. It has become quite popular in Western culture, and many gyms and fitness centers offer classes. Sign up for one today; you'll reconnect with your womanhood and feel empowered after your first class . . . if not a bit sore. Belly dancing is quite a workout on your abs, which is another great reason to try it.

218 Grow a Vegetable Garden

Growing a vegetable garden is easier than it seems. Even if you have just a small piece of land, that's a great place to start. Till the soil so it is loose and free of large rocks. If you want to section the space off, lay some bricks or a wood border along the perimeter. You can buy seeds or plants that are just starting to grow from a home improvement or gardening store. Place them in a row and use a marker that says what is planted there so you remember. Each seed packet or plant should come with directions on how much sun and water it should receive and when the best time to plant is. In a few months, you will have wonderful fresh and all-natural vegetables. Share them with your friends or neighbors. At the end of the season, when you've put the garden to bed for the winter, continue to throw vegetable scraps into it. You'll be surprised when you find that the seeds bloom in the spring. It's like getting free veggies!

219 Have an Acupuncture Treatment

Acupuncture is an ancient Chinese medical treatment that has been practiced for centuries. It involves inserting and manipulating small, thin needles into different areas of the body for the purpose of relieving pain and stress. The areas of the body where the needles are placed follow the meridians where qi or chi, vital life-force energy, flows. People get acupuncture for a variety of health reasons, even to get pregnant. Find an acupuncturist in your area to get a treatment. Let them know where your pain is and what you would like to accomplish with acupuncture. Do some research before your first visit so you can ask questions.

220 Sell Your Ex's Stuff Online

Breakups inevitably come with the separation of belongings, but more often than not each of us ends up with some hanger-on items we don't really know what to do with. Instead of feeling sad or nostalgic every time you spot his guitar in the back of your closet or her favorite painting in your garage, go on eBay or Craigslist and sell it to the highest bidder. Then, take the cash and buy yourself a drink—toasting to the fact that you've moved on. Way on!

221 Sculpt with Playdough

You probably spent more time trying to eat playdough than making sculptures when you were a kid. It was salty and smelled funny, but it was magical in its own way. Now that you're a bit older, you can still have fun molding it into jungle animals or flowers. Buy a few jars and create a wonderful sculpture. Or you can make your own, by combining flour, water, salt, vegetable oil, and a little food dye. If you have children, let them make it with you. If they want to eat it, you'll know it's safe.

222 Visit an Amusement Park

Spending the day on roller coasters and eating cotton candy will make you feel like you don't have a care in the world. Take a trip to your nearest amusement park today. Look for coupons on the Internet before you go to try and save some money on admission. The total cost of food can cost almost as much as another ticket, so do yourself a favor and bring your own lunch. You can enjoy some time away from the crowds and have a picnic. If it's a hot day, take advantage of the water rides, and be sure to bring an extra set of clothes to wear home. Be careful to stay hydrated and carry reusable water bottles. Enjoy the rides and the atmosphere, and you'll feel like a kid again.

223 *Bake Christmas Cookies in July*

. . . or whenever else you need some cheer! Sometimes, a year can be too long to wait for the tasty treat of Christmas cookies. Try to make a variety of cookies, like sugar cookies, gingerbread men, or peanut butter blossoms. If you can find cookie cutters in the shape of snowmen or Christmas trees, use them to make fun shapes. Buy different kinds of decorations like gel, frosting, sprinkles, and colored sugar crystals. You'll enjoy the tasty finished product and the very act of making them will fill you with holiday spirit—no matter what the calendar says!

224 *Hold a Reunion*

You might not be able to wait until your ten- or twenty-year reunion to meet up with old high school friends, so plan one yourself. Make a list of everyone you would like to invite. If it's been a long time, find your yearbook to refresh your memory. With social networks like MySpace and Facebook available, it should be easy to track down old buddies. Finding them will be half the fun. Get a reservation at a restaurant or bar in your hometown so everyone can come back to where it all began. Take a walk down memory lane and realize how easy you had it in high school.

225 Adopt an Endangered Animal

With the destruction of the tropical rainforest and the melting of polar ice caps by global warming, more and more animals are quickly becoming endangered. Through the World Wildlife Fund, you can adopt an endangered animal today. You can choose from hundreds of animals like polar bears, penguins, blue whales, and toucans. WWF will send you a plush version of the animal you chose, an adoption certificate, and a photo of your animal. You can donate as much or as little as you want. If you decide to get this as a gift for your child, remind them that they don't get to take the animal home. Go to *www.worldwildlife.org* now to adopt your favorite animal.

226 Bake Your Own Bread

With just a few simple ingredients, you can have a warm loaf of bread baking in your oven, making the house smell divine. Look for recipes online or in a cookbook. If this is your first time making bread, start with an easy recipe. Be sure to pick up bread flour and yeast at the grocery store. To make your life easier, invest in a bread machine. These wonderful gadgets can mix, knead, and bake a loaf of bread in about three hours. All you need to do is put the ingredients in the machine and press a button. Make your favorites like white, wheat, rye, and pumpernickel. Or try cinnamon raisin for breakfast or garlic herb when you are making an Italian dinner. There's nothing like the smell of fresh-baked bread to make your home feel warm and inviting. Once you start making homemade bread, you'll never want to eat store-bought bread again!

227 Organize Your Computer Files

Just as we do spring cleaning in our closet, attic, or garage, we must keep our computer organized as well. Start with deleting those files that aren't needed anymore. Make sure all files are in folders as opposed to thrown all over the desktop. Look up your disk size and keep an eye on how close you are to the maximum. Check on any updates that need to be installed to help maximize your computer's productivity. Finally, give your screen a nice wipe down. Knowing that your computer is clean and organized will give you an accomplished and peaceful feeling. Don't forget to back up your work!

228 Listen to Classical Music All Day

Some people believe that listening to classical music will make you smarter. Even if it's not true, some classical music can definitely make you feel more relaxed—a little Bach or Beethoven can do the trick. Today, only listen to classical music. You may find that you feel calmer and stress-free throughout the day. This works especially well if you are in rush-hour traffic on your way to or from work.

229 Wish Upon a Star

Legend has it that if you wish upon a star, your dream will come true. If it is a clear night, go outside and find the brightest star in the sky. Think about something you truly want, something very special. Find your star and wish out loud for your dream to come true. Put aside all reservations and negative thoughts that this is useless. Believe that what you want you will receive, and agree to do something kind in return. Thank the star for helping you and wait and see what happens. If you believe in your wish, it will come true.

230 Have Sex in Water

Have an aquatic adventure and get busy in the water. Whether it's in a pool, lake, the ocean, or the shower, having sex in water can be a lot of fun. There is one obstacle to face when doing it in water: it washes away natural lubricant. You will need to be prepared with a silicon-based lubricant to get the job done. Another great thing about being in the pool or ocean is that you are practically weightless, so getting into unusual positions is much easier. Try it out today.

231 Make Your Home More Energy Efficient

Going green is all the rage, and so is saving hard-earned money. Do both, and make your home more energy efficient. Replace all of the light bulbs in your house with compact fluorescent light bulbs. They use one-fifth the energy of regular light bulbs, saving you a significant amount on your electricity bill each month. Remember to turn off the lights when you leave a room. Plug up drafts using door snakes and plastic on your windows in the winter. Invest in a programmable thermostat. With the heat you save, the thermostat will practically pay for itself. Taking these simple steps will make your home more green and will make your wallet happy.

232 Make Your Own Body Oil

Using body oil is a fabulous after-shower regimen to keep your skin moist and smooth. Just like any bath product, body oil can be pricey. You only need three ingredients to make your own, so why not try it? Natural beauty products are better for you and the earth. You will need:

- Grape seed or sunflower oil
- Essential-fragrance oil
- A small bottle

You can get essential oil at your local holistic or metaphysical shop, and you might be able to find it at a health-food shop. Do a test to make sure you aren't allergic to the oil before you make your batch. Fill the bottle two-thirds with the grape seed or sunflower oil. Then put drops of the essential oil in until it is strong enough for you. This will be different for everyone, so add it drop by drop. Shake the bottle well. Your body oil should stay fresh for six to twelve months. Body oil is great for people with dry skin, so make some for friends and family as well.

233 *Decline a Wedding Invitation*

Weddings can be fun—you get dressed up, enjoy some tasty food and drinks, and maybe hit the dance floor. But they can also be the opposite of fun—awkward conversations, crappy banquet food, and dealing with drunks. Next time you get a wedding invitation you're not feeling, send your regrets and a gift, then spend the evening doing something that makes you happy. No formalwear required!

234 *Color*

As a kid, you probably spent hours coloring with markers, crayons, and colored pencils. You would try to be very careful to stay in the lines. Coloring can still be a fun and relaxing activity. Go out and buy your favorite coloring tool, whether it's a sixty-four-pack of crayons, thin markers, or colored pencils. Pick up a coloring book as well. Spend the afternoon coloring away. You won't have to worry about staying in the lines now, so that should take the pressure off.

235 *Go Skydiving*

Ever thought about throwing yourself out of a plane just so you can parachute to the ground? This extreme sport is getting more and more popular for those that want to push the limits. If this is your first time skydiving, you will probably want to go tandem. This means that the experienced instructor is attached to your back and controls everything; you are just along for the ride. Many people who skydive continue to do it over and over again because the experience is so unique. It's the one way to really feel like you are flying. Find out where you can skydive in your area, and face your fear today.

236 Buy Your Favorite Candy on Halloween

Remember counting and sorting all of your candy after trick-or-treating as a kid? There were always a few pieces that you really didn't like, so you would try to trade them with your brother or sister. Now that you are in charge of the treats, buy all of your favorites. Go to the store and don't hold back. You can't have too many Snickers, Reese's Peanut Butter Cups, Kit Kats, and Twix. Maybe you won't get any trick-or-treaters, and you'll have a big bowl of delicious candy to enjoy all by yourself. In case you get wiped out by the kids, hide a bag or two under your bed for emergencies.

237 Take Ballroom Dancing with Your Partner

Imagine gliding along the dance floor with the ease of Fred Astaire and Grace Kelly. Dancing used to be the most popular activity for couples to do on a Friday or Saturday night. With television shows like *Dancing with the Stars* becoming more and more popular, ballroom dancing is in the spotlight again. Convince your partner to take classes with you to rekindle the romance. It's a great way to get in shape and build confidence.

238 Take a Walk at Sunset

When the sun sets, it's time to wind down from your busy day. Take a relaxing walk in the park, on the beach, or even just around the block. Reflect on the good things that happened today and say thank you. If you have a nice view of the sunset, stop and appreciate the beautiful colors it leaves in the sky. It will help you relax, and you'll be able to get some exercise in before the day ends.

239 Make Your Own Ice Cream

The easiest way to make homemade ice cream is with an ice cream maker, and many of them can be found for under $100. When you make your own ice cream, you know it will be fresh and all natural. You can add any ingredients you want: fudge, nuts, peanut butter, berries, or vanilla beans. Try to think of the most outrageous flavor you can make. This can be a fun activity for the whole family.

240 Clean Up Your Personal E-Mail

Last time you checked, how many e-mails were in your personal e-mail account? How many of these were spam? Do you feel cluttered? Take time to delete these unneeded e-mails. If they are spam, make sure to mark the sender's address as such to avoid them coming in and filling up your mailbox. Create folders to file e-mails that you want to keep, such as "Need to respond" or "Photos." Don't forget to delete your spam and deleted folders when you are finished.

241 Be Late for Work

Call your boss this morning and let him know you will be a little late. Use that little bit of extra time to do something nice for yourself. Make a delicious breakfast, do some yoga, have sex, or take the dog for a longer walk. Sometimes, it can seem like we're always rushing around, so this morning take all the time you need. You won't be stuck in traffic on your way to work, and chances are you'll have a much more pleasant day.

242 Take a Yoga Class

Yoga is an ancient Indian practice that has become very popular around the world as both a physical and spiritual practice. By using methods of breathing and postures, yoga is believed to improve overall health, reduce anxiety, promote relaxation and flexibility, and increase self-awareness. Almost all gyms and fitness centers now offer yoga classes to the public—sign up for one today. If you aren't familiar with yoga, try a beginner class like Hatha yoga. You will practice breathing and do simple stretches and postures. Every yoga instructor will tell you not to do more than you are comfortable doing. Go at your own pace and focus on matching your breath with the movements. You will come out feeling refreshed and centered.

243 Cook Dinner Naked

Whether with your partner or alone, add some real spice to your meal by cooking it naked. If you have close neighbors, make sure your blinds are closed to avoid those peeping eyes. Plan to cook one of your favorite meals, but think twice about fried food, as a splash of hot oil will definitely leave an unpleasant burn. You may want to wear a skimpy apron to protect you from the hot appliances. Try a taste test with your partner . . . without using your hands. It usually gets pretty hot in the kitchen when preparing a meal, so why sweat in your soup—get naked!

244 *Make Your Own Candles*

If you really enjoy burning candles, buying them can become expensive. Consider recycling extra wax you have left over to make new candles. Collect all of the extra wax you can find left in jars that have burned down. Scrape the wax out of the jar and use a double boiler to melt the extra wax bits together. Use an empty candle jar to pour the new wax into it. Be careful not to burn yourself during this process. Now all you need are new wicks. You can pick them up at any craft store. Blend different scents together to create a signature candle. You can give them as gifts for birthdays or holidays.

245 *Wear Matching Undergarments*

Did your mom teach you to wear clean underwear in case you get hit by a car and have to go to the hospital? Well, this indulgence takes it one step further: Buy a matching underwear and bra set. It doesn't have to be lace or see-through or animal print, something simple can still be beautiful. Even if no one sees it but you, you'll feel sexy knowing you look good underneath your clothes . . . and your mom will be proud.

246 Sign Up for an Obstacle Course

Even the most dedicated gym-goers can sometimes find it hard to find the motivation to exercise. Why not give yourself a fitness goal and have a blast while doing it? Obstacle course races are increasing in popularity, and they're a fun way to get your blood pumping. Search online for obstacle races near your city or town, and have a blast climbing, jumping, and racing to the finish line.

247 Build a Sand Castle at the Beach

You are never too young to pull out that shovel and pail and get to work. When you are at the beach with your friends or family, have an adult contest for who can build the best sand sculpture or castle in an hour. Elect somebody nearby to be the judge, preferably a child. Whichever team wins should take the others out for a drink or dinner. Even if you are not making it a competition, relish sitting at the water's edge and watching your masterpiece come to life.

248 *Go Snowboarding*

Sliding down the slopes on a snowboard is a rush of excitement as well as a challenge. If you already know how to ski, you might have a better advantage than if you've never tried a winter sport. However, with the right instructor and plenty of practice time, you'll become a pro. Wear all of your protective gear and stick to the bunny slope at first. Don't be afraid to fall down; in fact, expect it. Those bumps and bruises can be cared for as you're drinking hot chocolate in front of a fireplace in the lodge.

249 *Go Ice Skating on Christmas Eve*

After setting out the milk and cookies, grab your skates and hit the ice. Take to the ice the night before Santa arrives for some needed stress-relieving exercise. You will need to relax from all the last-minute shopping and preparation for the holiday. You can head over to your local skating rink or try to find a pond that has frozen where others are skating as well. If you are not the greatest skater, the laughter that comes from the constant falls and slips has been proven to reduce stress hormones. Don't forget your gloves!

250 *Celebrate TGIF*

Thank God It's Friday! We all need to celebrate the end of a long workweek. Get dressed up and go out on the town tonight for some drinks and dinner. Make it a date with your honey or get a group of friends together to cause some trouble. See a movie or a show at the theater. Keep that Friday feeling going into the wee hours. It's the beginning of your weekend, so celebrate it!

251 *Plant a Tree*

Go to your local nursery today and pick out a nice tree for your yard. There is an endless variety of trees to choose from. There are evergreens, flowering trees, fruit trees, and ornamental trees, just to name a few. You can even buy a tree online and have it shipped to your front door. Check out *www.arborday .org*. You may decide to plant this tree in honor of someone who has passed away recently or even for a newborn in your family. It is a great story to tell when the child grows up and sees his tree, tall and proud, in front of him. You will not only add beauty and shade to your home, but help clean the environment's oxygen. Get planting today!

252 Drink Warm Apple Cider

Warm apple cider on a cool fall night will heat you up in no time. Pick some up at your local grocery store or at the nearest apple farm. To spice it up, add some cinnamon sticks to the pot. If you want to add a kick, add a shot or two of brandy. Grab your cup of cider, sit on the porch, and watch the leaves fall from the trees.

253 Create a Filing System for Important Documents

You can purchase a full-size filing cabinet or any of the plastic filing systems at your local office supply store. The plastic systems come in all sizes and price points. Some are small enough for receipts and others are sized for contracts and full-size legal paper. Go through your files and keep important tax forms, pay stubs, and loan information. Create a small table of contents for easy reference. Remember, this system will only help you in the end, and taking time now will save you a great deal of stress and worry later on.

254 *Make Up Baby Names*

Your children's names might be something you've already thought about, even if you don't have kids yet and aren't pregnant. It can be a lot of fun as well as a timesaver, so you know one thing's already done before the baby comes. Think of names for both boys and girls. Try to make them unique or special for your family. Incorporate names of relatives or names passed down in the family, but add a new twist to them. Make a list of all the names you like and try to narrow it down.

255 *Spend the Day with Your Pet*

Studies have shown that owning a pet can reduce stress and provide excellent health benefits. If you spend just a few minutes petting your dog or cat, your mood improves, blood pressure goes down, and breathing becomes more relaxed. Having a pet that needs to be walked means you are getting exercise, as well. They also offer a way for you to meet new people by going to a dog park. Today, spend the whole day with your pet. If you don't have one, ask a friend if you can take their dog for a walk or relax with their cat. Or consider adopting a pet from your local animal shelter.

256 Have Anonymous Cyber Sex

If you are feeling randy today but want to stay in the comforts of home, try a cyber adventure to spice things up. There are numerous chat rooms and websites where adults can meet up. Be wary of providing any private info such as your telephone number or hometown. It is always more sexy to be discreet, so make it more interesting and go by a fake name and age to help with the fantasy. Better to keep the webcams out of the fantasy; online videos last forever and you would not want that one time to end up out there in the infinite world of the Internet.

257 Feng Shui Your Home

Feng shui is a Chinese practice to help you improve your life by placing things in a certain order. Feng shui enthusiasts believe that the arrangement of the furniture and objects in their home will help them achieve their goals. The placement of these objects affects the flow of chi, or life-force energy, in an environment. Using colors in certain rooms and having walls in certain areas can affect the energy in your home. Do some research online to find out how to apply feng shui to the particular setup of your home.

258 *Power-Walk at the Mall*

The mall is a perfect place to get some exercise. Malls are usually made up of at least one or two floors with long corridors. You can do it by yourself, in a group, or as part of a program. According to Wikipedia, The Mall Walker's Association of America is one of the most popular mall-walking programs in the United States. Many malls open early for mall walkers, so you'll have it all to yourself. When you are done walking, you can treat yourself to a new article of clothing or book as a reward.

259 *Volunteer at an Animal Shelter for the Day*

If you love pets but can't have one due to rental restrictions or a family member's allergies, get your cuddle time in by calling your local animal shelter and asking if you can volunteer to work there. You may end up scooping a poop or two, but you might also take the dogs for a walk or just spend some quality time giving them love and affection.

260 Have a Snowball Fight

If you need to get out some pent-up stress or aggression, what better way than to throw some snowballs. Make sure your snow is not filled with ice, as you can really hurt someone if you are not careful. Get your friends together and make teams—see who can avoid those whipping balls of snow. Play it like dodge ball, but allow ten minutes for each team to build a fort or protection wall they can hide behind. Although you are acting like kids, remember you are adults and make sure to aim for nonfragile areas. Have fun and don't get hit!

261 Go Parasailing

Parasailing may look and sound like a wild ride, but it is a very relaxing experience. The more popular type of parasailing is in the ocean off a speedboat. Once strapped in, you're hoisted high above the water, trailing behind the boat. While riding, you have a beautiful view of the ocean below and the landscape of the shore. Parasail in the more tropical areas where the water is clear and you can see the coral reefs and marine life below. If you are lucky enough, you may see a passing dolphin or sea turtle. The cost of parasailing usually runs about $100 a person and will vary in different locations; however, it is truly worth the expense and the memory will last a lifetime.

262 Make a Haunted House for Neighborhood Children

On Halloween, trick-or-treaters think you are cool if you give the best candy, like full-size Snickers bars. This year, take it one step further and construct a haunted house for them to go through before they get their candy. You can do it on the front lawn, or if you are friendly with most of the families, inside your house. Play spooky music and set up games for them to win before they can move on. Decorate with spider webs, gravestones, fake blood, and hanging bats. However, don't make it so scary that the young ones can't enjoy it.

263 Eat Out on a Wednesday

It's the middle of the week and all you can think about is the weekend. It seems like it's taking forever to come. Now is the time when you need an unexpected treat to get you over the hump. Instead of waiting to eat out this weekend, choose a restaurant for tonight and change things up. You'll be able to eat leftovers for lunch tomorrow. Find little ways to get you through the week and you'll be much happier.

264 Walk Out on a Jetty

If you live close to the ocean, spend some time walking out on a jetty. Remember to walk and not run, as there are plenty of gaps and holes between the rocks where you could lose your footing. As you walk farther out, you will begin to notice that the buzz of the street is washed away by the crashing waves and the passing boats. Once you get to the end, you almost feel as though you are surrounded by water. This is always a great place to sit back and read a book or the newspaper. If you are in the mood for some excitement, bring your fishing rod and fish in the open ocean.

265 Make Homemade Hot Chocolate

Sure, it's easy to pour a packet of instant hot chocolate mix into a cup and add water, but nothing compares to a cup of rich, homemade hot chocolate. You'll need the following ingredients:

6 ounces milk
Chopped or shaved chocolate—you can use milk, dark, white . . . whatever you like
Sugar (optional)—the more cocoa content your chocolate has, the less sweet it is
Whipped cream, cocoa, cinnamon (optional)

Pour the milk into a saucepan and add the chopped chocolate until you have the desired taste. When all the chocolate has melted and the milk is steaming but not boiling, take it off the heat. Add some whipped cream to the top and a pinch of cocoa or cinnamon. Cocoa has been shown to have a lot of antioxidants, so drink up!

266 Make a Scrapbook for the Year

For a whole year, try to collect movie-ticket stubs, birthday and holiday cards, pictures, receipts for big purchases, headlines from newspapers or magazines, or anything else that will help you pinpoint the exciting moments of the year. Buy a nice scrapbook and create either collages of the seasons or journal pages with illustrations around the words. Capture the uniqueness of each year so you can look back and relive those wonderful memories.

267   *See a Broadway Show*

Seeing a show on the stage has been a favorite pastime for hundreds of years. Live theater can be magical with the costumes, stage design, music, and lighting adding to the ambiance. If you've never been to a show, look for one that might interest you online or in your newspaper and get tickets today. Shows can be expensive depending on where you sit in the theater—seats in the balcony are considerably cheaper than those in the orchestra. Sometimes, if you show up right before a show starts and they have extra seats in the normally expensive section, you can get them for a cheaper price. See if you can get a deal.

268   *Get a Photo of Your Aura*

An aura is the energy field emanating from and surrounding a body or object. Everything has an aura; some people can see them naturally while others can be trained to see them. They give off different colors depending on the frequency at which they are vibrating. The color aura you give off depends on your physical, emotional, and mental state. Auras can be documented by what is called Kirelian photography. Visit your local metaphysical shop to see if they will take a photo of your aura. If they can't do it there, they can probably recommend someone who does.

269 Take a Pole-Dancing Class

Why not kill two birds with one stone and shed some weight while feeling ultra sexy. You will be surprised to see how many fitness centers and dance studios offer pole-dancing classes. Whether you are wearing your five-inch stilettos or your beat-up gym sneakers, you will get an incredible workout and increase your confidence. If you are too shy to take a group class, you can purchase your own pole for your home and work out to a DVD. Carmen Electra offers the "Electra-Pole" at *www.electrapole.com*, complete with a DVD explaining the step-by-step assembly.

270 Plant a Rose Bush

There's nothing prettier than a rose. A whole bush of them in your backyard will make it look elegant and romantic. If you want to plant more than one bush, try to have a variety of colors like white, red, pink, and yellow. Plant your roses in direct sunlight—they need about six hours to thrive. They also need plenty of water, so be sure that they are planted in well-drained soil. Don't let the soil dry out. Prune them regularly and buy special sprays to keep away bugs and diseases like mildew. In the winter when they are dormant, cover them in burlap and tie it with string. This will protect them from cold winter winds and snow. Being able to smell the sweet rose fragrance every day is worth the steps you need to take to protect them.

271 Get a Wax

Do you have a few stray hairs in places you don't want them? Go to your local beauty salon and get a wax. Whether it's your upper lip, eyebrows, chin, or back, a wax will leave you smooth and hair free. Don't feel embarrassed about your unwanted hair; everyone needs a good esthetician now and again and the professionals have seen it all. You will walk out feeling confident and beautiful.

272 Take the Time to Unsubscribe

Unless your e-mail address is very new, you're probably on a whole bunch of e-mail lists whose messages you never even open. If you find yourself spending a few minutes a day deleting the clutter, why not sit down and spend ten or twenty minutes to remove your name from all those unwanted lists? The next time you log in to your inbox, you'll be glad you did it when the only messages you see are the ones you actually want to read.

273 *Have an Adult-Themed Scavenger Hunt*

What better way to feel like a kid than to have a scavenger hunt? Gather your twenty closest friends and create teams of three or four people each. Each individual will need to submit at least one task for the groups to accomplish. Make them creative but not too hard; you want it to be more fun than difficult. Create tasks like taking a picture with a Kama Sutra book or buying fifty blue jelly beans. Choose a nice Saturday afternoon for the hunt and set a meeting place to start and finish. Put a time limit on the hunt to keep the pressure building. If you are not in the city and will need to use gas, make sure your team has a designated driver and full gas tank.

274 *Kayak in the Ocean*

The crashing waves, saltwater splashing your face, and wind whipping through your hair; a kayak ride in the ocean is fun because it's a little dangerous. A kayak is a one-person watercraft, so you will be the one in control, pushing through the waves. You can ride together in a group, but you are in charge of paddling and steering the kayak. Find a place that rents kayaks or gives kayak lessons and spend the day at your favorite beach paddling away. Take in the scenery and look for fish. If this is your first time, try to take the kayak out when the seas are a bit calmer and remember to wear your safety vest.

. . . .

275 *Take a Haunted Hayride*

Haunted hayrides at Halloween can be really creepy. You are out in the middle of a field, in the back of a hay truck with a bunch of other people looking to be scared. If this ride isn't made for little ones, you'll probably come in contact with a chainsaw-wielding maniac chasing your truck. You'll encounter all sorts of scary situations, and it's all out of your control. It can be even more fun if you get a group together so you're all on the same truck.

. . . .

276 *Join an Adult Intramural League*

Whether you prefer dodge ball, baseball, bowling, or mini golf, there is an adult intramural league for almost every sport. This is a great way for singles to meet some potential mates or for couples to create another circle of friends. Most leagues are inexpensive to join and include a basic uniform. If you miss those days of organized sports and the camaraderie during and after the game, here is your way to get some exercise and release some stress after a long day at work.

277 Canoe Down a River

Enjoy a peaceful canoe ride alone on a calm morning or with a friend in the bustling rapids. Use this time to take in the beauty of nature around you and get in some good exercise. When choosing a canoe to rent or buy, specify your needs so you get the right canoe for you. Will you be alone or with up to six of your friends? Are you taking a day trip or a week-long adventure? Whatever the trip, a canoe ride is always a rewarding adventure and will help you truly enjoy the incredible serenity of nature.

278 Concoct a Crazy Combination at Cold Stone Creamery

Go nuts and try to create the most absurd combination of sugary goodness at your nearest Cold Stone Creamery. Cold Stone Creamery allows you to blend your ice cream with endless amounts of sweets such as butterscotch, candy bars, gummy bears, and sprinkles. It is blended by one of the workers on a frozen granite stone that keeps the ice cream cold and hard.

They have blended options such as Coffee Lovers Only, Our Strawberry Blonde, Peanut Butter Cup Perfection, and Cookie Mintster. Forget about the calories and dig in. Go crazy and create a new blend; maybe yours will become one of their signature creations!

279 Buy a Dry-Erase Calendar

Why waste the money and paper on a new calendar every year? If your plans change or dates get canceled, you can simply erase and start over rather than having a marked-up calendar with scribbles all over. If you are sharing this with your family or partner, pick a different color marker for each person so their schedule is clearly marked. By erasing every month that has passed and starting a fresh one, you can plan out your month and begin to see where you have your free nights and weekends to enjoy some needed relaxation.

280 Drink an Expensive Bottle of Wine

Tonight, clear your schedule and your responsibilities. A night alone, just you and a bottle of wine, will provide the getaway your mind needs. Purchase a nice, vintage wine out of your price range and plan to drink it all tonight. Put your pajamas on, pop in a romantic movie, cook a delicious meal for one, and drink away. Before you go to bed, drink a couple glasses of water and pop a few aspirin or vitamin C tablets to avoid the inevitable groggy morning hangover.

281 *Take a Tai Chi Class*

Tai chi is a form of martial arts that has been practiced for centuries. Created in China, tai chi is a slow form of martial arts that promotes health and reduces stress. Using flowing movements and steady breathing, tai chi has been known to lower blood pressure, increase circulation and flexibility, and is perfect for people with limited mobility. According to the 2007 USA Sports Participation Study, tai chi is one of the fastest-growing fitness and health-maintenance activities in the United States. Find a gym or martial arts studio that offers classes and take one today. You will enjoy the soft music and movements and will feel an overall sense of well-being.

282 Try a New Position

If you are caught in a rut under the sheets and your sex life is feeling bland, spice it up with a new position. It is healthy to communicate how you feel about your sex life to your partner and find ways together to improve your experience. There is plenty of literature out there that describes, and in most cases depicts, different positions that help stimulate each of you. Don't be afraid to ask a friend for some inspiration. You will be surprised to find that many couples are looking for interesting ways to stir things up in the bedroom but are too scared to admit it. Try researching a few new positions today and surprise your partner tonight.

283 Make Your Bathroom Shine

One of the most important places to keep fresh and clean is your bathroom. Take pride in keeping it sparkling clean, as this is the one place where you wash away the dirt and stress from the day and rejuvenate your body. Start with emptying everything out of the bathroom, including any cabinets. If you are holding on to your hotel collection of shampoos and body wash that you will never use, throw them out. Declutter and then begin cleaning. When you can see your reflection in the tiles, you have accomplished your goal! After putting everything back, add a nice photo or painting to the wall and your favorite scented plug-in or candle. Make your bathroom your oasis!

. . . .

284 *Get a Chair Massage*

Chair massages are perfect when you need a quick rubdown, like on your lunch break. In anywhere from five to thirty minutes, this blissful massage will loosen your tense muscles and let you float away from your stress. You sit in a specially designed massage chair with your face on a padded face rest. Your massage therapist should already do this, but make sure they put down a piece of paper towel or disposable tissue before you put your face down. If other people are getting massages, you don't want to transfer germs and bacteria. Your massage therapist will focus on your key tension areas, like arms, neck, back, and shoulders. Ask to have your head massaged as well—this will melt away tension fast. When you are on the run but still want to pamper yourself, opt for a chair massage. Sometimes you'll even see therapists giving them at the mall, perfect when you need a shopping break.

285 Schedule a Standing Lunch Date

We've all been guilty of skipping lunch or wolfing down our food while at the computer at work. But lunch is an important time to recharge yourself so you're ready to take on the afternoon. If you find yourself working through lunch more often than not, setting a standing date will make you more likely to get out of the office. Whether you're meeting a friend from the office or your husband or wife at a nearby restaurant, you'll make the time to have a meal and clear your head if you know you have a weekly or monthly date.

286 Go Sledding

You have the memories and the pictures to prove you enjoyed the thrill of sledding down a big slope on an inner tube or sled when you were younger, now relive the thrill. If you don't have kids, you probably don't own a sled or tube and need to purchase one. Sleds can run anywhere from $30 to over $200, but for a basic sled or inner tube, try to keep it under $75. Be aware when shopping that you will have an overwhelming amount of options compared to twenty years ago. Get bundled up in your snowsuit, let go of your inhibitions, and throw your hands up as you swish down the snowy slope.

287 Visit a Renaissance Faire

Huzzah! Today visit a local renaissance faire. They can be found all over the country, but if you don't know where one is in your area, check online. Dress up in Renaissance garb like busty corsets and velvet cloaks. If you've never dressed up before, you might feel silly, but most of the people attending will be dressed up, so you'd be silly not to! Order turkey legs for lunch and drink mugs of mead. Enjoy the jousting and other medieval games like shooting arrows or throwing hatchets. You'll feel like you've gone back in time and will get lost in the fun.

288 Deliver Christmas Gifts to Needy Families

Become involved with a local organization that delivers Christmas gifts to needy families in your area. Most programs will ask for volunteers to donate their car to drive around to designated homes to deliver presents. The smiles you will put on every parent and child's face will stick with you forever. The experience will remind you what the holidays are about, and to not be so focused on that flat-screen TV you are wishing for. If you can't make the delivery day, purchase a few gifts to donate to the cause. Make the holidays a time for giving back to those who are not as fortunate as you.

289 Have a Cheese and Wine Party

Invite a few friends and family over for a wine and cheese party. You may be celebrating a birthday, housewarming, or the weekend. Designate a region of the world to each guest and instruct them to bring a bottle of wine and cheese from that location. If any of your guests do not drink alcohol, have them bring a sparkling juice or cider that connects with that region. As the host, provide the crackers, appropriate utensils, and some small desserts. Remember, your television should not be the focal point of the party, as it deters from the gathering and breaks up the conversations. As the party winds down and wine is almost gone, stay away from the truth-or-dare game, as it could get ugly.

290 Go Pumpkin Picking

Whether you are in search of the perfect pumpkin pie or jack-o-lantern, go pick your own pumpkin. If you are looking for a decoration pumpkin, try to find one with the stem still attached and with the fewest bruises. The outside of the pumpkin should feel hard and be bright orange in color. Planning on baking? Ask for the sugar pumpkin, which is best for cooking. They are smaller in diameter, but check it out for rot or soft spots as well. Pumpkins will keep for a few months if you store them in a cool, dry place approximately 50°F–65°F. Instead of rushing to your local grocery store, make a day of it and find the best pumpkin out there!

. . . .

291 Incorporate Chocolate Into Every Meal

Try not to make this an everyday activity, but forget the diet today and get your chocolate fix. Chocolate has been proven to provide antioxidants, calcium, and iron. For you health nuts, stick to the dark chocolate, as studies show that it is better for you. For breakfast, try some melted chocolate and peanut butter on an English muffin or shaved Hershey's Kisses on your afternoon sandwich. Try some chocolate gravy for those biscuits and mashed potatoes, and don't forget your hot chocolate for an after-dinner dessert. Need some inspiration? Watch the movie *Chocolat*, where she creates an entire meal with chocolate.

. . . .

292 Get Your Car Detailed

Want to have your car look and smell brand-new? Take it to your dealer or mechanic to be detailed. This is more than just getting your car washed; every nook and cranny, inside and out, is given great attention and will sparkle when finished. Getting this done once a year will make you feel like you're driving a new car, even if you can't afford one right now.

293 Spend the Weekend with Your Favorite TV Series

Put aside your weekend chores and curl up on the couch with your favorite television show. You can rent almost any series now through Netflix or your local movie rental store. A weekend of *The Walking Dead*, *House of Cards*, or *Orange Is the New Black* will take you away from the real world, if only for a few days. If you want some company, invite some friends over that are also fans of the show and ask them to bring the appropriate beverages and snacks.

294 Hug Three Different People

When we were little children, we got hugged all the time. As adults, we don't receive as many hugs as we should. Hug three different people today to get your daily dose of human touch. Many people are uncomfortable with touching someone else. These days, you can't just touch anyone—you might have a sexual harassment suit on your hands—so know who you are hugging and make sure you have permission. Studies have shown that just being touched reduces anxiety, slows heart rate, and speeds illness recovery. We've all felt or given a superficial hug: no real embrace and a quick pat on the back. Be mindful of that and give a real hug: both arms around the other person and a firm squeeze. At the end of the day, notice if you feel more relaxed than usual.

295 Make Time for a Quickie

Studies have shown that having sex can better your overall health and help with the longevity of your life. They have found that even a romp in the sheets twice a week will reduce risk of heart disease, reduce depression, and improve bladder control and overall fitness. Isn't this enough of a reason to make time for a quickie? Even if you are too tired or too stressed, a quick ten- to fifteen-minute session can do the trick. It will definitely take the edge off a rough day and give you the quick jolt of energy you need to clean the dishes. Try it today, just before leaving for work or before dressing up for dinner tonight. Throw on your birthday suit and keep it quick!

296 Fill a Room with Lighted Candles

If you are thinking about cutting down on your electric bill or just want a romantic evening at home, fill an entire room with lighted candles. It would work best with unscented candles, as too many of the same scent would be overwhelming and a mixture could create an unpleasant smell. Choose a variety of shapes and lengths to create different heights and brightness of light. If this is for your lover, you may also want to sprinkle her favorite flower petals on the floor or play her favorite soothing music. The natural, flickering light will relax your mind, calm your senses, and create a beautiful ambience for your home.

297 Buy New Makeup

You might not think about this on a daily basis, but your makeup can go bad pretty quickly if not stored properly. It has a shelf life, just like food does, so check the labels on your makeup and replace any old products today. Liquid makeup—lip gloss, mascara, and foundation—goes bad faster than powders, and brushes and applicators are a breeding ground for bacteria. Every time you brush your face and then put it back into the makeup, you are transferring bacteria. Wash and sanitize brushes regularly to keep the germs away. Keep a log of when you buy your makeup so you know when to replace it.

298 Adopt a Pet from a Rescue Shelter

Having a pet in your home may be work, but the benefits always outweigh the accidents on the carpet and scratched furniture. There are so many abandoned animals that need a good home, and if you love animals, you should treat yourself to their companionship. Going to a pet store or purchasing direct from a breeder can burn a hole through your wallet. Instead, visit your local animal shelter today to see if a furry friend is right for you. When you take your new pal home, you'll know you made the right decision.

299 Build a Tree House

If you had a tree house as a kid, you will remember the fun times you had hiding from your parents or having sleepovers with your friends. As an adult, you may want to use this as your place of solitude or a tree fort for your own kids to enjoy. Remember to pick a sturdy tree to build the house. If you plan on using this as your getaway space, decorate it with anything that relaxes you, but remember, it will probably be exposed to the natural elements.

300 Backpack Across Europe

Plan your trip across Europe today. Research how much money you will need for any train, plane, or bus travel as well as accommodations. Create a savings plan with your partner or friend so you will be prepared for your trip. If you are planning on roughing it and staying at hostels, make sure to ask around in each city for the best accommodations. It is recommended to travel through Europe for about a month during the summer, as most hostels and museums are open. Unfortunately, there will be the inevitable long lines and higher prices. Try not to plan out an itinerary, as this will take the fun out of the adventure. Create a general plan of attack, but take the risk and fly by the seat of your pants. Enjoy the journey of a lifetime!

301 Celebrate First Night in the City

Ring in the New Year with thousands of your neighbors at First Night. Take the trip into a nearby city and enjoy the festivities it has to offer. Many cities will have events going on all day leading up to the stroke of midnight. Check to see if there is an all-access pass that allows you to see the ice sculptures or private concerts. Go with your close friends or family so you have lots of people you love to hug and kiss when the New

Year begins. If it will be a cold night, don't forget to bundle up, and remember to bring the confetti!

302 *Speed Date*

If you are done with searching for eligible singles at your friends' weddings or local bar, try a speed-dating event. There are organizations all over the country that sponsor these get-togethers at local restaurants and lounges. In most cases, the event will be broken down into age groups and even different ethnicities. You are usually given about five to ten minutes with approximately ten potential mates. Some organizations will have you go online after the event and enter who you are interested in meeting up with again. If it is a mutual connection, they will provide you with each other's contact information. If you are about to give up on love, stop and try a new approach. You owe it to yourself!

303 *Go on a Whale Watch*

Experience the extraordinary creatures of our ocean and go on a whale watch. If you have never been, you must experience this at least once. Depending on your location, whale watches may not run year round, so make sure to plan ahead.

Wear comfortable rubber-soled shoes and sunscreen and bring along a sweatshirt, even on a warm day. Most trips will last about two to four hours and will have snacks and beverages on board to purchase. The enormity of these mammals reminds us just how small we are and helps us appreciate our place on this earth.

304 *Have Dessert at the Cheesecake Factory*

Why go to the Cheesecake Factory and fill up on the entrées and appetizers? Save the room for some delicious cheesecake. There are endless options, including Brownie Sundae Cheesecake, Key Lime Cheesecake, or Chocolate Peanut Butter Cookie-Dough Cheesecake. If dinner was too filling, make sure to get a piece to go for later. Make sure to enjoy each and every bite and ignore the calories for tonight!

305 *Take a Staycation*

If you've never heard of one, a staycation is the same as a vacation, but you stay at home. You don't fly off to a Caribbean island or go on an expensive, lavish holiday. With troubling economic times, a staycation is the best way to save a few bucks while enjoying some much-needed time off. Think of all the things you can do while at home or close to home: You can decorate that second bedroom, visit the park or zoo, bake cookies, have friends over for a party, swim at the beach, and spend time with your family. The importance of a vacation is to have some downtime and recharge your batteries. What better location to accomplish both of those than home. You won't have to worry about lost luggage, missed flights, bad room service, or tourist traps. Plan your staycation today!

306 Catch Up on Celebrity Gossip

Sometimes we need an escape from the daily stress and to be a voyeur of someone else's life. Try to limit your gossip viewing, whether online or in your favorite magazine, as this should just be frivolous eye candy on your lazy afternoon. With so many popular gossip websites, like www.perezhilton.com and www.tmz.com, many people find themselves wasting time at work checking on the latest celeb to enter rehab. Give yourself a time limit if you begin to notice you are getting hooked. Enjoy your adventure into celebrity la-la land, but make sure to call it quits before your dinner burns in the oven.

307 Do Something That Scares You

Being afraid of something can hold you back from making life-changing decisions or improving your character. How will you see the world if you are afraid to fly? How will you get that dream job if you are afraid to move? Facing your fear will boost your confidence and open new doors in your life. Today, make the choice to confront your fear head-on. If you are afraid of heights, take an elevator to the top of a skyscraper and look down. If you are afraid of water, ease your way into a pool or the ocean. Nothing should hold you back from accomplishing your dream. Forget fear and move forward!

308 Watch Porn

Whether you are looking for some soft-core late-night premium-channel viewing or more of the fetish variety, porn is readily available and even free. There are numerous video stores that carry adult material to rent or buy. The Internet has also become a very popular place for your viewing pleasure. Although the pay-for websites usually offer a virus-free environment, there are also free websites such as www .xtube.com. Make sure to do your research and ask around for some reputable recommendations to avoid the sometimes disastrous computer viruses. Many will not admit to viewing the adult websites, but studies show that "sex" is the most searched word on the Internet. Click away and have some fun.

309 *Buy a Hot Tub*

Although this is a very expensive purchase, many will say this investment is truly worth the price. Your options are endless, and you can spend as little as $2,000 or as much as you want. Hot tubs are not only a great way to relax, they also help with relieving muscle tension, better sleep, and increased blood circulation. Keep in mind that there is a great deal of maintenance that goes along with these thermo spas, especially if they're outside. Do your research and decide which option best fits your needs. This may be a purchase you will need to save for, but the benefits truly outweigh the cost.

310 *Get Adjusted by a Chiropractor*

Many chiropractors offer a free consultation before you get an adjustment. The chiropractor will take a look at your spine and will take some x-rays. By looking at them, he will see where you are subluxated, where your spine is out of place. Chiropractics is based on the theory that subluxation interferes with the body's natural ability to heal itself and is the leading cause of all disease. By manually manipulating the spine, chiropractors put the spine and vertebrae in correct position. Our spines can get out of whack by sitting at a desk all day, sleeping, walking, and driving. Some chiropractors believe that we are subluxated the moment we are pushed from our mother's birth canal. Many insurance companies don't cover chiropractic care in their plans, so if yours doesn't, ask if you can get a free adjustment to see if it is right for you.

311 *Abandon a Book Without Finishing It*

Life's too short to waste it reading a bad book. Rather than finishing a novel you're not enjoying, liberate yourself from the guilt and abandon it before you're done. Ask a friend, librarian, or local bookstore employee for a recommendation for a new book to try, and keep on going until you get one you love.

312 Comfort Yourself with Southern Food

If you have had a bad day at work or an argument with your lover, it is time to eat some comfort food. It is said that chefs cook comfort food with a lot of love and butter! Whether it's a warm dish of biscuits and gravy or country fried chicken, Southern comfort food will give you a warm and fuzzy feeling inside and definitely make your soul smile. For some savory dishes, visit www.pauladeen.com and check out how she finds a way to fry almost anything. Remember, comfort food usually involves a great deal of butter and fried food, so make sure this is not an everyday occurrence. But for today, dig in!

313 Go Whitewater Rafting

For a truly thrilling experience, go whitewater rafting with a group of friends. Navigating the rough waters might be scary at times, but with an experienced guide and some training beforehand you should be safe. Be sure to wear your helmet and life preserver at all times in case you fall out of the raft. Enjoy the spray on your face and the exciting dips and turns on the choppy water.

314 *Make Your Own Christmas Wreath*

Decorate the front door of your apartment or home with a festive Christmas wreath that you made yourself. Invite your friends over to make their own to take home. You'll need the following items:

Christmas tree cuttings
1 Styrofoam wreath frame
Holly and pinecones
Red ribbon

Cut all the greenery to the same length and begin pressing them down into the Styrofoam. Take the holly and pinecones and begin pressing them into the Styrofoam in the desired locations. You can use a hot glue gun to help secure them if they are not staying in place. Finally, take the ribbon and make a nice big bow to place on the wreath.

315 Organize a Family Reunion

If it's been more than five years since your whole family has been in one place, it is time for a reunion. Send out a save-the-date to make sure everyone is available to come. Family can be funny and try to back out of these parties, but make sure to speak with each and every one of them. To ensure their attendance, ask them to bring a specific entrée or dessert. Ask everyone to send a family photo that is current and one that is at least five years old to create a then-and-now collage for everyone to enjoy. The location of the party should be an equal distance for everyone to help on gas. Make sure to take a group photo at the end and e-mail it to everyone so they can have it for their photo albums. Family is important, and sometimes it just takes a slight nudge to get everyone together again.

316 Have a Bonfire

Before having a bonfire or backyard fire, speak with your local officials about permits and regulations. Many areas have specific times of year that you can and cannot have a fire. Once you have the proper permit, and following all local rules, pile up any wood, sticks, and brush that are not needed and fire it up! Someone should be appointed the fire marshal to keep the fire contained and safe at all times. Sitting around a fire with friends and family makes for a fun gathering. Pick up some s'mores kits and savor some gooey marshmallows. If the air is crisp, sip on some hot chocolate or warm apple cider.

317 Enjoy Seasonal Beer

Seasonal beers concentrate on seasonal ingredients and specialize in the flavors of the time of year. These beers can sometimes be a one-time release, so it is fun to go for the moment and try them out. Brewers tend to make these beers to be enjoyed with the food of the season, so try to stick with a holiday specialty when accompanying the beer. Sam Adams makes a special brew for every season. Check out www .samueladams.com for a list of all of their varieties. However, you can't go wrong with a Corona with a slice of lime in the summer.

318 Start a Side Business

If you've always wanted to start a side business, now is the time. Maybe you have a great idea for a new product or business. Maybe you would like to make some extra cash off your favorite hobby. Come up with a business plan and figure out how it will work. If you make wonderful desserts, start small by selling them in the neighborhood. Create word-of-mouth advertising and watch your business grow. Build a website to promote your product or service; in this day and age, no matter what your business is, it needs a website.

319 Read a Book from a Different Genre

Books are a wonderful way to escape your world and dive into another. When you enjoy a certain type of story, you usually stick to that genre. Today, find a book that you never thought of reading. If you only read romance, choose a science fiction novel. If you really enjoy crime thrillers, try reading a memoir. It's great when you can find books that really grab your attention and pull you into the story. Don't get stuck in one category when there are so many to explore—try something new every now and then. You'll be surprised at how much is out there and how your tastes can change.

320 Pray

Whether you call it praying or taking a moment to reflect, remember to be thankful for the blessings in your life. Try to block out five or ten minutes every day—when you wake up or go to bed—to speak to your higher power. You may talk out loud in the car or rest silently in bed. Either way, take these moments to share your fears, hopes, and dreams. This daily activity will help you stay focused on your journey and continue to keep you grounded. Try writing your prayers into a poem or song or drawing them as pictures. However you feel you can best express your true feelings, allow them to shine every day.

321 Flirt Shamelessly

Get out there today and meet some potential mates. Whether you are at a bar, house party, or your local coffee shop, try to flirt with as many people as possible. Try to pick out those unhitched singles in the room and start up a conversation. Before the approach, try to think of something you may have in common to ease into the banter. Keep your discussion light and fun by avoiding any political debate or controversial topics. Keep your options open and make a goal of getting at least three phone numbers by the end of the night!

322 *Buy a Piece of Art*

Liven up your living space with a beautiful new piece of art. It can be an expensive sculpture or a cheap print of your favorite landscape. Choose something that will make for a conversation piece at your next house party, but one that you will enjoy year-round. You may decide to design your entire room around this one piece or match your art to the existing decorations. If you are stuck in the black-and-white theme, go for something with a lot of color to brighten up your room. Try to stay away from anything really busy for your bedroom, as this should be your place of rest. Purchasing any artwork or sculpture for your home will give it character and will make it feel like your own.

323 *Try a New Perfume or Cologne*

There are so many perfumes and colognes on the market with a wide variety of prices that you should not be wearing the same scent for more than a year. Switch your scent with the season as some perfumes or colognes better complement each time of the year. Go with a heavier, musky scent in the winter and a lighter, fruity smell for the summer. You can now design your own fragrance at certain stores and online to best complement your natural scent as well. Avoid bathing in your perfumes before leaving the house; you will get used to the smell, but a perfect stranger will sense you from a few blocks away!

324 *Haggle with Your Cable Company*

Cable television is one of the biggest drains on disposable income. If you're paying too much for cable (and who isn't?), call your provider and ask if there is anything that can be done to lower your bill. You might be surprised to find just how amenable they can be. Or, ask them if there are any ongoing promotions that allow you to try out a new movie channel or other service. The worst thing that will happen is they'll say no, and the best case is you save a few dollars on your bill every month—maybe while enjoying a movie from the comfort of your couch!

325 *Relax in the Sauna*

Whether after a workout at the gym or a long day at the office, let your body relax in the sauna. Studies says that sitting in a steam room or sauna can help increase blood circulation and help promote better skin, as the pores open up and release toxins. Use this time to meditate and relax your mind as well. Avoid thinking of the day's stress and the tasks that lie ahead and allow yourself to completely release that stress. Remember to drink plenty of water and do not exceed more than ten or twenty minutes per session. If you are unsure if a sauna is okay for your medical condition, always ask your doctor what is right for you.

326 Adopt a Different Persona for the Night

If you've ever wanted to be a different person, tonight's the night. Plan to go out to a bar or club and adopt a completely different persona. This isn't about lying to people; it's about having fun acting differently. Pretend you have a British accent or wear a blond wig if you have brown hair. See if people treat you differently. If you go out with friends, let them in on the secret so they can perpetuate it.

327 Make a Complete Thanksgiving Dinner for a Family in Need

This year, cook your entire Thanksgiving dinner for another family who needs it more. Work with a local food bank or organization to find a family in need. Have your family come over and cook with you to share in the experience. When you're done, pack up the dinner in nice containers and deliver them to the family. You may want to include decorative plates and napkins and plastic utensils. After you have delivered dinner, pick up some pizzas and enjoy some cheesy goodness with your family. You will all feel proud and humbled to know that a family is celebrating the way you have for so many years.

328 Take a Tour of a Factory

Ever wonder how your car was built or how your beer was bottled? Take a tour of the factories that make your favorite item and marvel in the process. Some of the more popular tours are the Yankee Candle Factory, Hershey's Chocolate Factory, or the Ben & Jerry's Factory. Don't forget the free samples and tastings directly after the tour has concluded. Bring a few friends and make a day of it. You will be surprised to see just how much work and energy goes into some of the simple things we take for granted in our everyday life.

329 *Watch a Lightning Storm*

Lightning is a truly incredible sight, and its sheer power is overwhelming. If you hear thunder, you are within striking distance and you should be indoors. The safest place to view a lightning storm is in your house. Try to stay away from the window, but position yourself so you can see out in the distance. If you happen to be in a car, make sure your windows are up. To stay completely out of harm's way, check out the beauty in the sky at www.youtube.com and search for lightning storms.

330 *Order a Mixed Drink You've Never Had Before*

Next time you are out to dinner or at the bar, jump out of your comfort zone and try a different drink. Go for a specialty drink or the one that sounds the most interesting. Impress your friends on your next outing by asking for this unique drink, and it may become your signature cocktail. If you don't want to go out and spend money, buy a cocktail recipe book or find one online to try out. Invest in a cocktail shaker to look the part at your next party.

331 *Get a Tune-Up*

Keeping your car in tip-top shape is one of the most important things you can do. You want to get as much life as possible out of the car and keep the large costs down, and getting a regular tune-up is one way to ensure that happens. Take your car to your dealer or a mechanic you trust and have them look everything over. Follow the recommended guidelines from your manual so you know what the car needs for its mileage. Have them check the brakes and tires and all of the spark plugs. Be sure to get your oil changed every 3,000–5,000 miles and rotate your tires every other oil change. Make sure your filters are cleaned as well. Wash the interior and exterior often. Taking care of your car will give it a longer life and will make you feel confident that you are safe.

332 *Make a Family Tree*

Discovering where you came from can give you great insight into who you are now. Trace your roots back by making a family tree. Ask relatives if they can help fill in the blanks or go online to try and find public records that might give you clues about family members who have passed away. There are many websites that can help you trace your ancestry, like www.ancestry .com. You can create your family tree right there and search for others on the website that you might be related to.

333 Make a Playlist of Favorite Songs from the Year

What better way to remember the year than by putting together a playlist of your favorite tunes? Include the songs that were the biggest summer hits or the ones that remind you of a special time. Ten years down the road, you will be able to place yourself in the exact moment you heard that song or it may bring up a few memories of the year gone by. You may want to create a photo slideshow using the playlist as a soundtrack that you could e-mail to your friends and family as a keepsake.

334 Go Jet Skiing

Have you felt the rush of the water skim by your ankles at over 40 mph? If you answered no, it is time to go Jet Skiing. The rush you get when you are out on the open water—whether on a lake or ocean—is incredibly releasing. You feel as though you own the waves and you have all the power in the world. Go with a friend, family member, or partner and you will never laugh so hard. Every bump, twist, and turn will have you screaming for more, and the moment the trip is over you will want to go again. Rental prices can range up to $200 per vehicle, and the rides usually last about an hour. Splurge on this one; you will love the rush!

335 Recycle

We hear every day how important it is to recycle, yet so many of us are too lazy to take a few extra minutes to go through with it. In many towns and cities, recycling is mandated. By recycling, we drastically reduce the waste sent to landfills and decrease the amount of energy used in the production of new products. By taking these few extra moments in our day, we will not only make our world a better place, but the next generation's as well. Take a moment today to educate yourself on how to properly recycle in your home and set a plan in motion to become more eco-friendly. We must take care of our world as it takes care of us. No excuses!

336 Wear Sunscreen

Protect your skin from the harmful rays of the sun by wearing sunscreen. No matter what level SPF it is, make sure to reapply at least two or three times during the day. Be especially careful during the midday hours when the sun is at its strongest. Remember to apply sunscreen at home or in the car at least thirty minutes before sun exposure to maximize your protection. Sunscreens with UVA and UVB protection are most effective in preventing skin cancer and other skin ailments. If you don't like the oily feeling on your skin all day, try to get an oil-free sunscreen. Allow your body to live a long and healthy life by protecting it when having fun in the sun!

337 Accept a Friend's Offer to Watch Your Kid(s)

When you first have a baby, people come out of the woodwork offering to help you out by watching the baby. Why not take them up on the offer? Call a trusted friend or family member who offered such kindness and tell them you'd like to make good on their offer. They may be surprised at first, but more likely, they'll be happy to help out. Then, enjoy a guilt-free couple of hours by yourself. Resist the urge to go grocery shopping or run other errands. Buy yourself a coffee and enjoy it at a park, or even take a nap in your bedroom while the kids are entertained downstairs. It's your time to rest and recoup!

338 Learn a Different Language

Most of us wish we had paid more attention in our required language classes in high school. Not only is it helpful when traveling, but on your resume it can add tremendous value when you can speak more than one language. Studies show that only 5.5 percent percent of the world speaks English as a primary language. You can take classes online, purchase a book, or take classes at your local college. Learning this new language will not only increase your global understanding, but will also open up new opportunities for you. There are more than 6,000 different languages in the world today, so pick one and start studying. Expand your mind!

339 Order One of Each from the Dessert Menu

When you are out with a friend and feel the need to satisfy your sweet tooth, overindulge and order one of each from the dessert menu. Give in to your temptation and allow yourself this break today. You may want to skip the entrée completely and focus only on the sweets. Sometimes, not following the rules and getting that awkward face from the waiter or waitress will give you that jolt of happiness you have been looking for. Eat the ice cream desserts first, before they melt, and leave the cakes and pies for last.

340 Write a Letter to Your Favorite Teacher

It is never too late to thank that teacher who truly made a mark on your life. He may have been the one who constantly told you to stop chatting in class or the one who took the time to show you how to do your multiplication. Reflect today on that one teacher who changed your life and get his contact information. Send him a letter thanking him for helping make you the person you are today. If you graduated recently, buy him your college sweatshirt and send it to him. When your teacher receives this letter, he will feel incredibly touched and inspired to keep educating others.

341   *Buy a Terrycloth Bathrobe*

Haven't you always wanted one of those fancy terrycloth robes that you find hanging in your hotel room? They are not that expensive, so go out and get one! Wrapping yourself in one of these robes after a warm bath or shower keeps the warmth in and allows you to dry off while relaxing as if you were at the spa. Buy one for your partner, too, but consider getting different colors or personalizing them with your initials. If monogramming is too classic for you, put each other's nicknames on the robes.

342 Try a New Class at Your Gym

There are numerous classes offered at your local gym, and almost everyone is intimidated to join until they try it once. Sign up today and try one out. You will notice immediately that many people feel the same way you do and have difficulty with similar exercises. Working out in a group also keeps you motivated, and you will begin to make a group of new friends that are all working toward a common goal. Most gyms will allow you to sit in on a class and watch for a little bit to decide if that level is right for you. Make working out fun and enjoyable and join a class today!

343 Learn How to Sail a Boat

Learning how to navigate any boat is one of the most rewarding and enjoyable experiences. If you love the water and want to spend some time on the open seas, take lessons. Learning to sail will usually cost anywhere from $500–$1,200, depending on where and how in depth the program goes. Most basic plans will teach you the parts of the boat and rigging, rules of the road, chart reading, and navigation. This is a great activity to do with your partner or friend so you learn as a team and share experiences. Make it a point today to research your options and even order a beginner's how-to-sail DVD to become more informed.

344 Go to a Free Wine and Beer Tasting at a Liquor Store

If you are on a budget and need to spend wisely, keep tabs on your local liquor stores. Many of them will offer free wine and beer tastings at the store. Instead of buying a whole bottle or six-pack, check out a few before spending your money and throwing out a bottle once you get home. If you think you will be tasting a few too many, make sure you have a designated driver to take you home. If you and your friends would like to have a tasting party, have everyone purchase a type of beer and wine that is unknown to the group and do it at home. Drink responsibly!

345 Try a New Hairstyle

Have you had the same hairstyle for the last ten years and are too afraid to do something drastic? Today is your day. Spend some time searching for your favorite haircut in magazines or people-watching at the mall. Keep this a secret from your friends and family so you don't cloud your head with their opinions, and surprise them at your next gathering. Trying something new and different will make you feel refreshed and renewed and may even give you that needed boost of confidence. Remember, they can always go shorter but not longer, so tell your stylist to go slow so you can coach them along to your desired length.

346 *Buy a New Winter Coat*

Is your winter coat beginning to look like a rag? If it is, it is probably not keeping you too warm, either. Go out and buy yourself a nice winter coat this season. If you are on a budget, find a coat that you could wear to a dressy occasion as well as something casual. Always check to see how it needs to be cleaned, to avoid those expensive dry-cleaning bills. Department stores are a great place to start, as they usually provide a wide variety of lengths, colors, and warmth. The best time to buy a winter coat is usually at the end of the season, when everything goes on sale; however, the holiday sales are also a great place for a bargain.

347   *Make Your Own Potpourri*

Potpourri is a wonderful way to make your home smell fresh and clean, and it's also a great decoration. Make your own potpourri today. Take a trip to the craft store to collect supplies. Be thoughtful when choosing so you pick items that have a lot of color and texture. Potpourri should be visually appealing as well as fragrant. Pick fresh herbs and flowers or dried varieties—anything that smells nice together will work. If you are making it for the kitchen, try to use cooking herbs like rosemary and sage. If it's for the bathroom, try lavender and sweet pea. Pick ingredients until you blend the right combination for you. When you are satisfied with the smell, store it in a covered container for approximately four weeks to allow the scent to develop properly. Shake the container every three days to awaken the scent. After four weeks, pour it into a decorative bowl. Make some for holiday gifts or birthdays.

348   *Have a Séance*

Connecting with our loved ones who have passed on is something almost everyone tries to do. We are naturally curious about what lies beyond this life: Do we go to heaven? Do we watch and protect our friends and family? Do we reincarnate and start another life? We'll never actually know what happens, but it's good to be curious. Tonight, hire a medium to perform a séance for you and your friends. Ask everyone to bring an object that is somehow connected to someone they have lost. Keep an open mind and have fun. Accept any messages that come as signs of love from those on the other side.

- -

349 Have a Day of Compromise

Compromise is the key to a lasting relationship. Today, make a game out of it with your partner. Keep an egg timer around and set it for exactly an hour. For one hour, do something together that you want to do. Watch your favorite movie, go for a walk in the park, or take a nap. When the buzzer goes off, it's your partner's turn. Let her know she can pick anything: Have sex, eat junk food, play cards . . . anything is fair game. You may find out that you didn't know what her true hobbies were.

- -

350 Build a Gingerbread House

Building gingerbread houses around the holidays is a tradition for many families. They are not only great decorations or centerpieces, but make for a tasty experience while putting together. Many stores sell kits that provide everything you need to make a gingerbread house; walls, roof, frosting, and candy decorations are usually included. If you really want a challenge, try to make it from scratch. Use green gumdrops as shrubbery, peppermint sticks for a fence, white frosting as snow, and bars of chocolate for a driveway. Be creative, and try not to eat all of the gingerbread until the house is finished!

351 Get an Eye Exam

Don't take your eyesight for granted. If you have vision insurance, take advantage of it. You should have your eyes examined every two or three years if you are under the age of forty. It is important for your doctor to check for any problems or diseases that may not have any symptoms. We are only given one body and we must take care of it!

352 Take Flying Lessons

Afraid of flying? Ease that worry by learning what all those buttons and controls do in the cockpit. The cost of flying lessons are all over the map, and are sometimes determined by how much time you can commit to the study hours and class time. Do your homework before signing up with a specific training facility. Since learning how to fly can take a great deal of time and money, make sure this is something you want to learn and are willing to commit to. The feeling of soaring through the clouds and enjoying the beauty above will be an incredible experience.

353 Join a Walking or Running Club

If you need some motivation or just want some friendly company while taking your afternoon walk or run, join a club. There are many groups and clubs that you can join for little to no cost. A volunteer coach will help instruct you on healthy ways to prepare for a marathon or for a simple brisk walk to keep your body toned. Running or walking with a group is always helpful because you can carry on a conversation, and before you know it, you have reached your goal distance. If you want to keep track of your times and routes, there are plenty of computer programs and devices that can assist you in tracking your progress.

354 Have a Yard Sale with Your Neighbors

If you want to clean house and make some extra cash but feel that you don't have enough to have your own yard sale, gather your neighbors together. Each of you should plan on posting fliers in different areas of town to help spread the word. Throw some burgers and hot dogs on the barbecue to feed those hungry shoppers. You may consider making this an annual event and get your whole neighborhood in on the fun. Avoid mixing your stuff with your neighbors so dividing money doesn't become a problem.

355 Get a Spray Tan in the Winter

Want your skin to have that sun-kissed glow throughout the winter months? Try a spray-on tan! This new technique not only keeps you out of the tanning booths and harmful UVA and UVB rays of the sun, it makes you look like you just stepped off the beach. Many say the process feels like you are in a car wash, but in only a few seconds you have a safe and perfect tan. If this is not for you, try some of the self-tanning lotions or bronzers. You may need to experiment with a few before you find the right one, so take your time and don't give up. Take care of your skin and get a healthy tan in seconds!

356 Buy New Shoes on Your Lunch Break

You can never have too many shoes, as most women will tell you. They can be addictive, so get your fix on your lunch break. If you're having a rough day at work, do something nice for yourself even if you really don't need another pair. Splurge on a new pair of heels, sandals, boots, or slides. Get something really special, not just a pair of sensible black shoes. Shoes can make an outfit, so buy some shoes first and build an outfit around them. You can pick up new clothes on your next lunch break!

357 Throw a Time-Capsule Party

Invite your friends or family over for a time-capsule party. Ask them to bring one item that either represents them or is significant to them. They may decide on a special photo, CD, or letter to themselves of hopes for the future. Designate someone who will promise to never open it and guard it as the keeper of the capsule. Decide as a group when you will open it again; it may be in five years or twenty. Whatever the time, it will make for two very fun and unique parties and a great way to switch things up!

358 Join AAA

Joining AAA is not just for the roadside assistance; you will be surprised to see how many discounts are available to you once you are a member. Whether it is a hotel, rental car, flight, train ticket, restaurant, zoo admission, or amusement park ticket, discounts are available. With this card in your wallet, you can feel safe in case of an emergency and get money off everywhere you turn. Visit www.aaa.com to check out the membership that is right for you as well as the incredible list of partners where discounts are available.

359 Enjoy a Facial

Take care of your skin and splurge on a facial today. Most facials will start off with a deep cleaning to unclog your pores and an exfoliation. The skin specialist will analyze your skin, advise you on what products are best for your skin type, and how to improve your home regimen. These treatments are proven to improve your complexion and increase circulation. If you want to save money and do it at home, there are plenty of lotions and nightly masks that you can buy at your local pharmacy. Light some candles and turn on some relaxing music to give yourself that spa experience. Reward your face with the attention it deserves today and treat it to a good cleaning!

360 *Eat Organic*

Eating food without pesticides, hormones, and fertilizers is better for your body and for the planet. Organic food has become increasingly popular in the past ten to twenty years, as people are becoming more conscious of what they feed themselves and their families. Visit an organic grocery store like Whole Foods or Trader Joe's today and do your weekly grocery shopping. Organic food tends to be a few dollars more expensive, but it is worth it. You know what you're putting into your body and you don't have to worry about anything unnatural.

361 *Sell Old DVDs to Buy New Ones*

Are your DVDs from ten years ago that you're still holding on to beginning to clutter up your shelves? Why not use them as cash to purchase your next set of movies? You can sell your DVDs on websites such as *www.amazon.com* or *www.dvdswap.com*. Hold on to the classics and your favorites. It is a safe bet that if you haven't watched a DVD in years and dust is growing on the case, you will not miss it when it is gone.

362   *Make a Zen Garden*

The purpose of a Zen garden, also called Japanese rock garden, is to have a space in your yard devoted to meditation and relaxation. Traditional Zen gardens are made of sand raked to make designs of circles and flowing, wavy lines. Less is more when it comes to being Zen, so large polished rocks, gravel, grass, and water are added to make it look simplistic yet beautiful. If you don't have a lot of space in your yard for a full garden, you can buy a miniature Zen garden that fits on your coffee table. It is a box of sand that comes with a small rake, stones, and Asian sculptures. You might have seen them in a doctor's office to ease anxiety. Raking the sand makes you feel very Zen.

363   *Invest in a Time-Share*

Time-shares are usually condos or rooms at resorts around the world that are owned by multiple parties. Each owner then gets to stay at the resort for a period of time (typically for one week a year). By investing in a time-share, you have a guaranteed one-week vacation spot for the year. You can even trade it to stay anywhere in the world. If you go away a lot for vacation, a time-share could be very beneficial. Look into the option of buying one today.

364 *Put a New Spin on a Family Recipe*

Cooking and sharing food with family is one way we show our love. Every family has traditional recipes that have been handed down for generations. Think of one that is a family favorite and put a new spin on it. If your family is famous for its lasagna, add sausage instead of beef. If your grandmother's chicken noodle soup is an old standby when you're feeling sick, add some different vegetables or use rice instead of pasta. By making it your own, you're creating new classics that can be passed down to your children and grandchildren. If you have a lot of family recipes to choose from, honor your ancestors by making a family cookbook and giving it as a gift during the holidays.

365 *Plan Your Dream Vacation*

Pretend that money is not a concern and your budget is endless. Think outside the box and plan out the most extraordinary vacation you can dream of. Make sure to include when you would want to go and for how long. Try to pin down the exact locations and what you want to see and do. When finished, write it down and store it somewhere safe. As life moves along, add to and edit the document. Take a look at it twice a year to remind yourself of this getaway. In a few years, you may be surprised at how much of a potential reality it has become.